VOYAGEURS NATIONAL PARK

Water Routes, Foot Paths, & Ski Trails

Jim DuFresne

**Additional winter research
by Steven J. Maass**

**The Mountaineers
Seattle**

THE MOUNTAINEERS: Organized 1906
" . . . to encourage a spirit of good
fellowship among all lovers of
outdoor life."

09876
54321

Published by The Mountaineers
306 2nd Avenue West, Seattle, WA 98119
Published simultaneously in Canada by Douglas & McIntyre, Ltd.
1615 Venables Street, Vancouver, British Columbia V5L 2H1

Book design and maps by Marge Mueller
Cover design by Constance Bollen
Copyediting by Sharon Bryan
Photos by the author unless otherwise credited
Manufactured in the United States of America

On the cover: (Top left) Ski touring in Voyageurs Park. (Top right) Kayaker on
Kabetogama Lake. (Bottom) Campsite at dusk on Namakan Lake. First photo by
National Park Service; last two by Jim DuFresne.

Library of Congress Cataloging in Publication Data
DuFresne, Jim.
   Voyageurs National Park : water routes, foot paths
& ski trails.

   Bibliography: p.
   Includes index.
   1. Outdoor recreation—Minnesota—Voyageurs National
Park—Guide-books.   2. Trails—Minnesota—Voyageurs
National Park—Guide-books.   3. Canoes and canoeing—
Minnesota—Voyageurs National Park—Guide-books.
4. Hiking—Minnesota—Voyageurs National Park—Guide-
books.   5. Skis and skiing—Minnesota—Voyageurs
National Park—Guide-books.   6. Voyageurs National
Park (Minn.)—Guide-books.   I. Title.
GV191.42.M6D84 1986 917.76   86-2468
ISBN 0-89886-110-1

CONTENTS

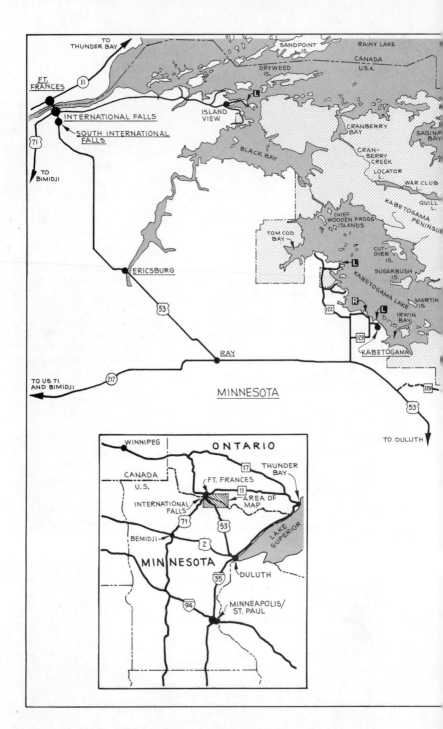

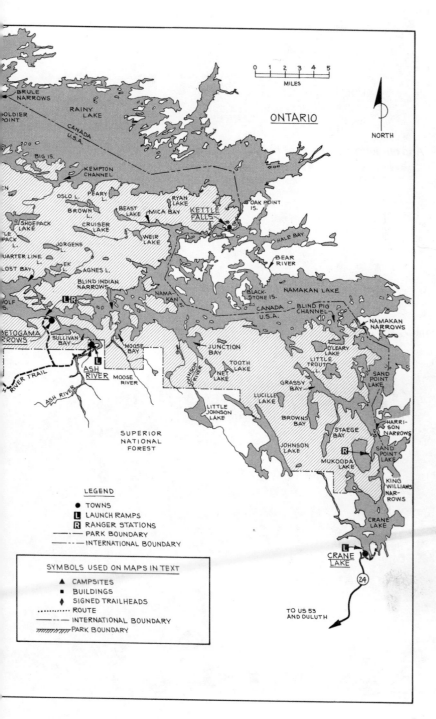

SYMBOLS USED ON MAPS IN TEXT

▲ CAMPSITES
■ BUILDINGS
♦ SIGNED TRAILHEADS
········· ROUTE
—··—··— INTERNATIONAL BOUNDARY
▨▨▨▨▨ PARK BOUNDARY

LEGEND

● TOWNS
Ⓛ LAUNCH RAMPS
Ⓡ RANGER STATIONS
—···— PARK BOUNDARY
—··—··— INTERNATIONAL BOUNDARY

To Rick

And our journey across the Kabetogama Peninsula. The brother I lost in the jungle, I found in the woods.

Hiker on inland lake (National Park Service photo)

FOREWORD

More and more visitors are discovering the waterways and trails of one of our nation's newest national parks, Voyageurs. This area had long been contemplated for national park status, even as early as 1891, for its outstanding lake scenery, geologic conditions and its waterway system. Once the home of Indians, loggers, gold miners, commercial fishermen, and voyageurs, the park has now become the destination for thousands seeking recreation. The waterways and landscape remain much the same as when the voyageurs plied these waters hauling supplies and trade goods west and furs to the east.

Visitors can find exceptional opportunities to canoe and camp in this lake country. Jim DuFresne's guide to the foot paths, ski trails and canoe routes in Voyageurs is detailed and complete. Jim spent most of one summer with a kayak investigating every bay, channel and promontory of all the lakes and every conceivable portage between them. He walked park trails and hiked old logging roads, diligently covering the entire park, and taking detailed notes of each area. Steve Maass, a park employee, skied the trails to gather information for the winter section of the book.

Newcomers will find this guide, with its detailed route descriptions, invaluable in exploring the park. For those who know and love the area as I do and have spent many pleasant and happy hours exploring the waterways and trails in the park, this book will provoke memories and suggest new routes and campsites to try. Using this guide provides all visitors an excellent introduction to Voyageurs National Park.

Russell W. Berry, Jr.
Superintendent
Voyageurs National Park

Acknowledgments

Merritt Johnson loved his coffee. He lacked most luxuries at his park station on the Kabetogama Narrows, but he did have a drip pot and a can of ground, roasted beans. Every three weeks, when my supplies ran out, I emerged from the middle of the park at Merritt's cabin, counting on an evening of good coffee and warm conversation. Lengthy journeys into the woods do much to sharpen my senses and reacquaint me with nature's beauty. But they also rekindle my appreciation for the simple pleasures of life—things that so often get lost in the shuffle. Little pleasures like a cup of Merritt's coffee and an evening of stories.

Merritt's hospitality made my nine-week journey through Voyageurs National Park a memorable one. Many other people did the same, enriching my experience with their special insights into the park and its colorful history. Lee Grim, professor at Rainy River Community College and one of the most knowledgeable people about the park's back country, was one of them. Another was Chuck Campbell, a seasonal naturalist at the park who loves to share his passion for the French-Canadian paddlers who preceded him there. My research was also aided by Glen Cole, wildlife biologist; Gladys Cole, director of the Lake States Interpretive Association; Mary Graves, park librarian; and George

Josephs of the NOAA weather center in International Falls, Minnesota.

When I was in the park, many took the time to stop and give me extra supplies, a weather warning, or—in the case of Ranger Bruce Malloy—a steaming bowl of potato soup on a rainy night at Mukooda Lake. District naturalist Ron Erickson and seasonal naturalist Ron Schmid were welcome company during a hot afternoon on Rainy Lake, and summer volunteers Kari Iversen and Tammy Perkins traded a dinner for a brief kayak lesson. Simple pleasures, brief friendships, a memorable summer.

Superintendent Russell Berry and Assistant Superintendent Dick Frost enhanced my understanding of the park considerably with their thoughts on its past, its creation, and its future. Mary Jane Berrey aided me greatly at the park headquarters, researchers Hildy Reiser and Patti Connaughton at Hoist Bay, and Steve Maass with the winter portions of the book.

I would like to extend my appreciation to Donna DeShazo, manager of The Mountaineers Books, and my editors Steve Whitney, Ann Cleeland, and Sharon Bryan for being so patient with me. My deepest gratitude goes to Nancy Zwers for putting up with a writer on the run in the Windy City.

Then there are those who encouraged me to write the book: Chief Naturalist Bill Gardiner, who spent hours working with the manuscript; enthusiastic visitors like Donna and Barb Pietsch, who ordered copies before the first page was even written. Most of all I am indebted to three very special people: Tom Centlivre, Mike Cowan, and my wife Peggy. They are the ones who have always encouraged me to leave my boots in the woods and my heart in my words.

Safety Considerations

Hiking, skiing and canoeing in the backcountry entail unavoidable risks that every adventurer assumes and must be aware of and respect. The fact that a trail or route is described in this book is not a representation that it will be safe for you. Trails vary greatly in difficulty and in the degree of conditioning and agility one needs to enjoy them safely. Some routes may have changed or conditions may have deteriorated since the descriptions were written. Also, conditions can change even from day to day, owing to weather and other factors. A trip that is safe on a dry day or for a highly conditioned, agile, properly equipped hiker, skier, or boater may be completely unsafe for someone else or unsafe under adverse weather conditions.

You can minimize your risks by being knowledgeable, prepared and alert. There is not space in this book for a general treatise on wilderness safety, but there are a number of good books and public courses on the subject and you should take advantage of them to increase your knowledge. Just as important, you should always be aware of your own limitations and of conditions existing when and where you are traveling. If conditions are dangerous, or if you are not prepared to deal with them safely, change your plans! It's better to have wasted a few days than to be the subject of a wilderness rescue.

These warnings are not intended to keep you out of the backcountry. Hundreds of thousands of people have safe and enjoyable backcountry trips every year. However, one element of the beauty, freedom and excitement of the wilderness is the presence of risks that do not confront us at home. When you travel the backcountry you assume those risks. They can be met safely, but only if you exercise your own independent judgment and common sense.

(Opposite) Cormorant colony near Fox Island in Rainy Lake

PART ONE

VOYAGEURS:
THE NATIONAL PARK

Canoer at sunset on one of the large outside lakes (National Park Service photo)

1 A PARK IN THE NORTH WOODS

There is a high bluff on Rainy Lake, near Anderson Bay on the Kabetogama Peninsula, where you can see three days' travel by canoe. With a twist of the head, you can see over 50 miles of shoreline, two countries, and thousands of acres of open water. And at dusk on a calm day, when the wind disappears and the setting sun illuminates everything in deep yellows and burnt oranges, you can drift back 200 years or so and see the canoes. They are large 25-foot birchbark canoes with eight red paddles moving them easily through the waves.

These were the voyageurs, transporting trade goods to the far reaches of the Northwest in exchange for furs. And from this point, on days so calm and with a view so compelling, it is easy to drift back and envision those ancient paddlers.

The voyageurs were the main characters in an epic chapter of North American history. Their legendary feats of paddling for 16 hours a day and hauling 300 pounds of goods across a portage trail were the yardstick woodsmen measured themselves by 200 years ago. Today few outdoorspeople can comprehend such endurance, much less match it.

They were short, stocky French Canadians whose strength and love of the wilderness opened up the North Woods' beauty and wealth to the rest of the world. Like the land they conquered, they were robust, colorful, and unpredictable. Their paths into the Canadian Northwest were many. But no matter where they began or what trading post they were headed for, these spirited adventurers had one thing in common—they all funneled through Rainy Lake.

The French Canadians and their red paddles are long gone, but the lake remains and it seems only appropriate that today this special point overlooking this historic route lies in a place called Voyageurs National Park.

North Woods Mystique

Voyageurs National Park, located on the Minnesota-Ontario border just west of the Boundary Waters Canoe Area (BWCA), was given presidential approval in 1971 and opened during the summer of 1975. It is an infant in the National Park Service (NPS) compared to such established parks as Yellowstone, Grand Canyon, or even Isle Royale, its North Woods counterpart that was created in 1931.

Voyageurs is young, undeveloped, and unique as a national park. Four large lakes—Rainy, Kabetogama, Namakan, and Sand Point—form the boundaries of this wilderness, and Crane Lake is a major access point, making it the only water-dominated park in the NPS System. There are no roads into the park—all travel in and out of Voyageurs depends on the water, as it did during the days of the fur trade, when the French Canadians paddled a 56-mile section of the park.

There are 30 named lakes within Voyageurs; water constitutes 83,789 acres of the park's total of 217,892 acres. In the middle of all the water is the Kabetogama Peninsula, the wilderness heart of the park. A roadless land mass of 75,000 acres, the peninsula is 26 miles long and 7.5 miles at its widest point.

The topography of the peninsula and much of the rest of the park consists of rolling hills interspersed between lakes and poorly drained swamplands and bogs. Land elevations in the western and northern sections rarely exceed the outside lakes by more than 100 feet, but high points of 1300 to 1400 feet above sea level are common in the eastern half of the peninsula and along the south shores of Kabetogama and Namakan lakes.

The beauty of the park comes from its mixture of wide expanses of water, hundreds of islands, and rugged coastline along the outside lakes. The peninsula's north shore along Rainy Lake is exceptionally irregular, with numerous rock outcroppings and abrupt changes in elevation shielding dozens of narrow coves and hidden bays. The south shore, while not as rugged, features slabs of smooth granite that were polished by glaciers 10,000 years ago and today are used by visitors for camping, picnicking, or catching the warm rays of an afternoon sun.

Voyageurs is only the newest preserve in the Border Lakes region, a traditional destination for backpackers in the Midwest. The Superior National Forest, encompassing nearly three million acres—including the Boundary Waters Canoe Area—is located between Voyageurs and Lake Superior. North of the BWCA in Ontario is the 1.1-million-acre Quetico Provincial Park, and 150 miles east of Voyageurs is Grand Portage National Monument. Isle Royale National Park lies 20 miles farther east in Lake Superior. While the preserves of the Border Lakes region are managed by different agencies and divided by an international border, it would be next to impossible for visitors to look at a tree or study a bog and know which park they are in—or even what country. Nature pays little attention to our imaginary boundaries.

This book focuses primarily on Voyageurs National Park but also includes information on Kabetogama State Forest to the south, Superior National Forest to the east, and the Canadian Crown Lands to the north. Often a trip will begin in one and end in another, or start in the United States and swing into Canada before returning across the border.

For convenience of description the park and the surrounding area can be divided into six distinct sections as far as the visitor is concerned. Some will hum with activity during the summer, others will offer the solitude and isolation that so many cherish as a brief escape from their busy worlds at home.

KABETOGAMA LAKE: At 15 miles long and 4 miles at its widest point, this is the largest body of water that lies entirely within the park. Kabetogama is the easiest lake to reach, has a strip of 30 resorts along its southwest shore, and thus supports the most activity of any section in the park. There are 11 NPS primitive campsites on the lake. Four of them are in the scenic Lost Bay area at the east end of the lake, which is also the site of trailheads for Locator Lake, Jorgens Lake, and the Cruiser Lake Trail system.

RAINY LAKE: Easily the largest lake in the area, Rainy is 12 miles at its widest point and 60 miles long, of which 40 miles lie inside the park. The lake contains 2500 miles of shoreline and 900 islands, yet sees less visitor use than the more accessible Kabetogama. Rainy is often a favorite among experienced canoeists and kayakers. The rocky coastline along the lake's south shore is some of the most spectacular in the park. The lake also provides access to several trailheads to the interior of the peninsula, including the Cranberry Creek Portage to Locator Lake, trails to Brown and Peary lakes, and the northern terminus of the Cruiser Lake Trail system.

KABETOGAMA PENINSULA: This is the wilderness heart of the park and the site for most of Voyageurs' trails and portage routes. The major trail system of the park, the Cruiser Lake Trail, is here. It consists of 21 miles of trails which traverse the land mass from Lost Bay on the south shore to Anderson Bay on the

Sandy beach on Rainy Lake

north shore. Paddlers can enjoy several interior routes, including the Chain of Lakes, where portages connect Locator, War Club, Quill, and Loiten lakes with Rainy and Kabetogama lakes on the outside.

NAMAKAN LAKE: This crescent-shaped lake measures 17 miles from its west end where it joins Kabetogama Lake at Old Dutch Bay to the Namakan River in Canada at the east end. It is almost 3 miles at its widest point and contains 146 miles of shoreline. The American side to the southwest is a maze of islands, 104 of them within the park, that make up a variety of safe channels containing 36 primitive campsites, including 18 clustered around the scenic southeast shore near Namakan Narrows.

SAND POINT LAKE: This smallest of the four outside lakes is 7.5 miles long and 2.5 miles at its widest point. Sand Point is divided in one direction by Harrison Narrows and the other by the international boundary. The shoreline is broken by several deep bays on both sides of the border. Lying within Voyageurs is scenic Grassy Bay, with its high granite cliffs and its appealing side arms, Browns Bay, and Staege Bay, which are both popular with paddlers.

THE MAINLAND: South of Kabetogama and Namakan lakes is an area of numerous lakes and rivers whose jurisdiction is shared by Kabetogama State Forest, Superior National Forest, and Voyageurs National Park.

Within this area is the popular Ash River Falls Ski Trail, located in the northern part of the State Forest. The 12-mile trail system is used by hikers during the summer and is groomed and tracked for skiers in the winter.

Boundary Waters versus Voyageurs

There is little debate that Voyageurs lies in the shadow of the Boundary Waters Canoe Area. The BWCA is larger, older, and renowned throughout the country as a wilderness canoeing area. Few people outside of Minnesota realize that there is a national park west of the BWCA and even fewer are aware of the canoeing and hiking opportunities it offers. Those who do know of it might ask themselves why they should go to Voyageurs National Park when they could just as easily swing into the BWCA.

The answer is simple. The areas are different. They offer scenery, wildlife, and wilderness experiences that are unique and very much their own. Backpackers and paddlers should not choose one or the other, but eventually try to explore both areas.

Throughout much of the BWCA there are small lakes and limited views. But Voyageurs is characterized by its huge lakes, which offer sweeping scenes where you can watch the sunsets melt into a watery horizon. The hundreds of islands and rocky islets throughout the park inspired author Robert Treuer to call it the Aegean Sea of the North Woods.

The BWCA offers paddlers thousands of portage-linked lakes and streams and designated campsites where emergency help might be a day or two away. Voyageurs offers the other two extremes in backcountry trips. For those who have no desire to keep portaging their boats over trails, it is possible in VNP to enjoy two weeks' worth of paddling where you lift your canoe only to take it home. And paddlers new to the world of extended canoe trips often find it reassuring that NPS rangers patrol the large lakes. The other extreme is an unregulated, undeveloped tract of wilderness where it's possible to escape into areas that only the moose and wolves dare to go. Since Voyageurs back country does not now see heavy seasonal use, the NPS has not had any reason to institute reservation systems, nightly fees, or strict limits on cross-country travel and camping.

In Voyageurs National Park you can camp on any point, follow any ridge, or portage into any lake without writing months ahead for reservations, special permission, or even a backcountry permit. While most visitors are content to stay on the maintained trails, for some people the thrill of the outdoors is following an old logging trail or depending solely on their compasses to travel from one interior lake to another. For them Voyageurs is a rare gem in the National Park System—an area that has been preserved but not trampled by masses of humanity during three summer months.

Someday this may change. As this new park becomes an established park in 20 or 30 years, as more portages are built and more trails are planked, and as more people realize it exists, park administrators may have to enforce the rules, regulations, and limitations other parks now have in effect. But for now there are sections of Voyageurs that are as untrampled and hard-to-reach as they were when the canoes that passed by were made of birch bark and the paddles were bright red.

2 THE RECLAIMED WILDERNESS

Dick Frost leaned back in his chair, stared at the map of Voyageurs National Park on the wall, and rubbed his reddish beard. One question stumped him; it made him contemplate the map for a few seconds as if the answer were hidden between the contour lines.

"Is Voyageurs a wilderness?" he repeated to himself. "Does wilderness mean the original condition or a pristine natural setting? You can still go in the park and get a 'wilderness experience.' To that extent it's as much a wilderness as you're going to find. It's still wild on the peninsula, not domesticated. If wilderness is a historical term, if it means an area that has never changed, this park is not. But then, you won't find wilderness in a lot of national parks."

The phrase that is often used to describe Voyageurs country is "reclaimed wilderness." The area is not in the same untrampled state as when the voyageurs first paddled through 200 years ago. Human needs, wants, and greed have brought about major changes in its wildlife, fauna, and landscape.

The most notorious intrusion came from the extensive logging operations that lasted from the late nineteenth century until 1972, cutting practically the entire park. But the sturgeon fisheries and the short-lived gold rush stripped a resource and left their scars as well.

Somehow the land survived, and when Congress approved its national park status in 1971, the reclaiming began. The National Park Service bought private

Early photo of horses pulling sled of logs (Photo courtesy of Koochiching County Historical Society)

land, removed structures, and banned hunting and trapping within park boundaries. After several generations had marred the wilderness for profit, the current one has been determined to return it to its original state. But that may never be possible. The woodland caribou that once roamed here may never be back. But today you can drift in a canoe along the shores of Rainy Lake and see what the voyageurs saw, feel the wind they felt, understand that special love their hearts held for the North Woods.

Voyageurs National Park: The Oldest and the Newest

At one point during the Precambrian Period, perhaps one to two billion years ago, the area that is now Minnesota was the site of spectacular volcanic activity that gave rise to a high mountain range. Eventually ancient seas spread back and forth over most of the area to erode the mountains into plains of layered sediment. The sedimentary rocks were later altered into schist, slate, and other metamorphic forms.

Today this metamorphic bedrock is the foundation of the Canadian Shield, a vast land mass of Precambrian rock that forms the nucleus of the North American continent. Voyageurs National Park is located on the southern portion of the Shield and the metamorphic sediments and igneous intrusions it comprises represent some of the oldest rock formations in the world.

What makes the park geologically unique is that these formations are exposed at several locations within its boundaries. They appear as a belt of greenstone that runs west through the BWCA, touches the northern edge of Voyageurs, and continues northwest into Canada. Greenstone emerges from beneath the water at several points in the park, including Dryweed and American islands north of Kabetogama Peninsula and on the mainland at Neil Point.

The shape and land formations of Voyageurs and the entire Border Lakes region came from another era of geological time. The Ice Age, or Pleistocene Era, began two million years ago, when four continental glaciers ground southward. The last one, the Wisconsin Glacier, ended only 10,000 years ago and had the most profound effect on the park. This ice age lasted 40,000 years and exposed earlier Precambrian rock strata through its scouring and erosion process. The mantle that was scraped off in the Border Lakes region formed the fertile plains south in present-day Minnesota, Wisconsin, and Michigan.

In the park, where the ice worked the bedrock like a giant abrasive tool, the effects of the glaciers are easily seen in other ways. The irregular shoreline of Kabetogama and Rainy lakes is considered to be the result of the slow-moving ice "plucking out" the rocks and depositing them farther south. Other signs include long grooves on exposed sections of bedrock, rounded and smoothed rocks, and displaced boulders. The most striking example of the glacier's work might be in Cranberry Bay where a very rounded boulder that weighs in excess of 200 tons was deposited near the mouth of the waterway.

The glaciers also carved out the Border Lakes' magnificent system of interconnected lakes that range from Lake Superior to Lake of the Woods.

Geologists consider Voyageurs and the surrounding region a rare find. Side by side among the lakes, rocky shorelines, and in a thin layer of topsoil are signs of the most ancient geological times, the Precambrian, and the most recent, the postglacial. You can view 3½-billion-year-old sedimentation, touch the results of 10,000-year-old glaciation, or wander through the slow, postglacial healing of the land. The oldest and newest chapters of the continent are visible here.

The Arrival of Man

Frenchman Jacques de Noyon, who arrived at the Border Lakes region in 1688, is generally considered the first Westerner there. But he was hardly the first person to see it. Nor were the Sioux Indians, the area's inhabitants when Noyon paddled through, the first.

Archeologists believe the first people appeared in what is now Minnesota around 9000 B.C., after crossing the Asian–North American land bridge at what is now the Bering Strait. The earliest signs of humans in the park area come from the Archaic Tradition, seminomadic hunters whose remains have been found on three sites within Voyageurs and are believed to have existed from 5000 to 1000 B.C. They were followed by people of the Woodland Tradition, who became more permanent residents by using the land and its resources more fully.

By the time the first French explorers arrived the Sioux, and later the Ojibway, had developed a complex economy of gathering, fishing, and hunting. The cornerstone of their existence was wild rice, which made up a quarter of their diet. The tall plant flourished in the Border Lakes region, with its cool climate and abundance of water, and was so important that each family had its own rice patch to harvest year after year. They began the harvesting in August, using a pair of sticks to knock the ripe grain into a canoe. Later they dried it, parched it,

Indians gathering wild rice (Photo courtesy of Koochiching County Historical Society)

and danced on it to remove the outer husks, then stored it underground in birchbark containers for the winter.

With their rice secure, the Indians turned to fishing and trapping during autumn, broke down into small hunting parties for the winter, and rejoined into larger maple sugar camps come spring. The process of gathering and boiling down the sap lasted a month, after which the sugar was used for seasoning fruits, vegetables, rice, and fish.

The entire cycle and seasonal patterns of the Indians were made possible by one device—the birchbark canoe. It was more than just efficient transportation that allowed tribes to complete their yearly circuit of hunting, fishing, ricing, and gathering. The canoes also had a profound effect on the exploration of the North Woods, were the key to the great fur trade, and laid routes that would later become international boundaries. This simple boat, made of birch bark, spruce roots, and cedar wood, affected people and nations far beyond the Indians of the Border Lakes.

It is not known when the canoe was first developed, but it had been used by Indians long before European settlers arrived in America. Its design was ideal for the Border Lakes region—it was extremely durable, with a normal life span of 10 years, yet light enough to be easily portaged through this mass of lakes, and maneuverable enough to weave safely through roaring rapids.

It is ironic that the same technology that made it possible for the Indians to thrive in the area eventually put an end to their way of life there. The first French explorer to arrive was Noyon who paddled through in 1688 and built a wintering post on Rainy Lake. But the influence of the Europeans began long before the French Canadian pushed his way through Rainy Lake to Lake of the Woods.

The fur trade between the Indians and Europeans had begun soon after Montreal was founded in 1611. Before long competition for European goods became intense among Indian nations and led to the Iroquois conducting raids from their strong upstate New York base on fur-trading parties headed for Montreal and Quebec. By 1650 the Iroquois had driven west of Lake Huron the bulk of the Algonquians, a linguistic nation that was made up of several tribes including the Hurons, Cree, Cheyenne, Fox, and the largest family, the Ojibway.

Furs and the immense profit to be made from them were the key to opening up the North Woods by way of the Border Lakes region. Furs had been a sign of rank since the Middle Ages in Europe, and a luxury that was closely regulated by governments and the church. Some countries were quicker to profit from the fur trade than others: while the Spanish searched for gold in the south and the English developed commerce and colonies on the eastern seaboard, the French combined their search for the Northwest Passage with fur trading.

When the Iroquois drove other tribes away from Montreal and Quebec, the French took the trade to the North Woods and returned with the furs. The men who paddled into the Border Lakes region were called "coureurs de bois," or couriers of the woods. They were freelance trappers or traders who worked on their own and often without government approval. One of the most famous was Sieur des Groseilliers who in 1654 stunned Quebec's citizens by returning with a flotilla of 50 canoes filled with furs.

The French government, wanting more control over the trade and its profits, began to crack down on these couriers and in 1660 confiscated Groseilliers's furs from his next trip when he reached Montreal. While Groseilliers hurried to London to convince the English of the immense profit in furs, the French tried to gain more control over the industry by issuing licenses to a select group of traders. One man granted a license in the 1720s was Pierre Gaultier, sieur de La Vérendrye, when he promised to search for the Northwest Passage.

Along with his supplies, canoes, and trade goods, La Vérendrye took with him his four sons, 50 soldiers, and hired paddlers who would become known as "voyageurs." The party set off in 1731, following a hand-drawn map given to La Vérendrye by an Ojibway Indian. They arrived at what is now Grand Portage on the shores of Lake Superior, where the explorer sent one of his sons inland to winter at Rainy Lake. The son reopened the wintering post de Noyon had built at the head of the Rainy River. The following spring the main party arrived at the newly named Fort St. Pierre and continued to Lake of the Woods, where Fort St. Charles was erected.

How actively La Vérendrye searched for the Northwest Passage is uncertain, although he did explore past the Missouri River to the Rockies in 1742. What he did do was build a string of forts and wintering posts from Rainy Lake to Winnipeg that turned the fur trade into a solid industry. It became a profitable business run by licensed companies that did away with independent couriers by hiring their own voyageurs to paddle their canoes.

The Treaty of Paris of 1763, which ended the French and Indian Wars, gave England control of Canada and of the North Woods fur trade. The English wasted little time in abolishing all monopolies and licensing many traders in each area. The result was heated competition between the Montreal traders and those of the Hudson's Bay Company which developed its fur route from James Bay and the Hayes River.

In 1778 the Montreal and Quebec traders organized into the North West Company and the Border Lakes became the battlefield of an undeclared war for beaver pelts. Back in the fashion capitals of London and Paris it had been discovered that beaver fur is minutely barbed, so that it could be bound to cheaper hair of rabbit or cat to produce felt of considerable strength. The felt, which was molded and shellacked into several kinds of men's hats, became a status symbol and the rage of European society. Felt hats were such a trivial thing, but they propelled brave men across a continent to give Canadians east-west commerce 30 years before the Americans crossed the Mississippi River.

The French Canadian adventurer known as the voyageur was the backbone of the entire industry. He was recruited from small settlements along the St. Lawrence River from Montreal to Quebec and signed for a one- to three-year tour of duty. He was chosen for his short stature—there was no room in a freight canoe for six-footers; because he was strong enough to portage 180 to 270 pounds of furs at a carry; and because he could sing. Historian Grace Lee Nute, in her book *Voyageur's Highway*, explains why singing was a way of life to the voyageurs.

> The voyageur sang when he was happy, when he was in danger, when he got up in the morning, as he sat by his campfire at night, when passing through white water, when at his fort, and especially while he was paddling. He was an effervescent being who took life easily, worked hard, took orders well, assumed little responsibility, got on admirably with the Indians, especially native women, and gave a fine loyalty to his bourgeois. He was an excellent canoeman—better, in fact, than the Indian. His ability to live in the wilderness, made him the mainstay of the trade. And he was chosen in part because of his ability to sing.

In May of each year the 35-foot canoes, carrying up to 4000 pounds of trade goods, departed from Montreal with a crew of 12 voyageurs known as "mangers du lard," or pork-eaters. These men, whose diet consisted mainly of a mushy pea soup seasoned with salt pork, would paddle the open waters of the Great Lakes from Montreal to what is now Grand Portage. The trade goods would then be carried over the 9-mile Grand Portage Trail to Fort Charlotte, where the "hivernauts" or winterers arrived in 25-foot North canoes filled with the furs.

The voyageurs' route from Montreal to the furs in the Canadian Northwest spanned over 3000 miles, and was too long for a single brigade of canoes to cover in the short paddling season between break-up and freeze-up. The fur companies resolved this problem by having some men spend the winter in the interior. These were the *hivernauts*—experienced voyageurs who paddled east following spring break-up to meet the Montreal canoes at Grand Portage. They carried the furs along a route through the Border Lakes (including the 56-mile stretch that is now in Voyageurs National Park) to as far west as Lake Athabasca.

Even then it was impossible to paddle from Lake Athabasca to Grand Portage in one summer, so the North West Company built Fort Lac La Pluie, or the Rainy Lake House. The voyageurs from Lake Athabasca would stop at Rainy Lake House and hand the furs to a special brigade and then return to Lake Athabasca with the trade goods before winter freeze-up.

Rainy Lake and Rainy River were the key to the voyageurs' route. Every trader, whether he was English, French, or American, passed along the shores of Rainy Lake, and every major fur company, North West, Hudson's Bay, XYZ, and even the American Fur Company established posts here at one time or another. Rainy Lake House was often called the "rendezvous of all Athabasca."

The most famous rendezvous, however, took place at Grand Portage, where the hivernauts met the pork eaters and exchanged goods. During the heyday of the North West Company in the early 1800s, this was a month-long celebration of dancing, brawling, drinking, and business transactions. The North West Company partners, or "bourgeois," would arrive along with Montreal agents and hold formal balls and banquets in the great hall while outside the voyageurs and Indian men and women would dance in the glow of campfires.

The short period of jubilation and roistering at Grand Portage was a brief respite in an otherwise hard life. Voyageurs began their day with a predawn paddle on an empty stomach before stopping for breakfast, one of only two daily meals. Then they would continue well into the evening before beaching their canoes to make camp. Supper was often eaten by the light of the campfire as late as 10 o'clock. They paddled from 15 to 18 hours a day at 40 strokes a minute while kneeling among the bales of freight and rested only five minutes every hour to smoke their pipes.

They had little protection against the swarms of black flies, gnats, and mosquitoes that attacked them day and night, and were expected to push on in pouring rain, high winds, or cold weather. Only the ice-covered lakes of freeze-up would stop them. But the most dreaded part of the journey were the portages between navigable bodies of water, which meant unloading the canoes and hauling both boat and freight overland.

To carry the 90-pound bales of fur the voyageurs used a device called a tumpline that they borrowed from the Indians. A tumpline is a broad leather strap that wraps around the toter's forehead and down his shoulders to the bundle on his back. There were no shoulder straps or hip belts—only this piece of leather that brought the voyageurs' strong neck muscles into use. The men were expected to haul at least two 90-pound bales at one time, and often they attempted three. Those who traveled with the voyageurs and recorded their accomplishments were always amazed at the sight of one of them bent over with the weight of three bales. But they were stunned when he took off trotting down the trail. Voyageurs faced many dangers in their journeys, and lives were lost to overturned canoes, hostile Indians, jealous traders, and hypothermia. But just as many died from hernias caused by the portages.

These men not only understood the dangers of their profession, they gloried in them. They were rock-hard, intense men who thrived on the challenges and hardships found in the North Woods wilderness. To risk their lives—not to mention their cargo—running rapids that most men would portage did more than just save hours of sweat in an overland haul. It was their passion in life and fuel for their burning pride. Grace Lee Nute quotes one 70-year-old voyageur who put it best:

> For 24 (years) I was a light canoeman. No portage was too long for me. I could carry, paddle, walk, and sing with any man I ever saw. When others stopped to carry at a bad step I pushed on—over rapids, over cascades, over chutes; all were the same to me. . . . Were I young again, I should glory in commencing the same career. There is no life so happy as a voyageur's life.

After the turn of the nineteenth century the quest for furs became a heated affair between the Hudson's Bay and North West Companies. The furmongers had posts almost facing each other from Fort William on the shores of Lake Superior through Rainy Lake to Lake of the Woods and beyond. Covert bargaining by employees of both companies was common, as was the practice of using liquor to draw the Indian's business. Raids and seizure of furs and trade goods all along the route were a daily hazard.

The rivalry carried both companies to the brink of bankruptcy until the struggle ended in 1821 when Hudson's Bay swallowed the North West Company. Hudson's Bay prevailed because their route to London through the giant bay in northern Canada allowed the company to deliver goods and return furs at half the cost of their Montreal-based rival. When John Jacob Astor's American Fur Company arrived in the Border Lakes region and began building its own post on Rainy Lake in 1823, Hudson's Bay was eager to avoid another fur war. In 1833 the English company agreed to pay its American counterpart 300 pounds sterling annually on the promise that the American Fur Company would not conduct trade.

By then the fur trade was declining rapidly. A change in fashions, with hats being made smaller and out of silk, is the reason most often given for the death of the great fur industry. But it was only one of many factors that ended the days of the voyageurs. Beavers had been so recklessly slaughtered, with whole colonies being exterminated, that their low numbers made the animal much more susceptible to disease. Another factor was the financial panic of 1842, which sharply reduced the demand for fur. At the same time the Indians who supplied the pelts to the trading post were being pushed onto reservations and forced to give their lands to the U.S. government through one treaty after another. Soon fur traders found themselves without trappers.

By the 1880s, a hundred years after the Great Hall at Grand Portage had been built, the fur trade was dead. The red paddles of the voyageurs were gone and their songs, sung to the rhythm of their strokes, were to be heard no more on Rainy Lake.

Blueberries, Black Caviar, and White Pines

The land that includes what is now Voyageurs National Park and northern Minnesota changed hands four times from 1671 to 1803 as Spain, France, England, and the United States all laid claims to it. It took decades before the area was surveyed and the boundary firmly mapped out, but according to historian Grace Nute, the Americans didn't need an exact border to confirm something they had begun to suspect in the 1850s—that their northern neighbors were stealing their trees. Canadians were swinging south, illegally cutting the superior white pine on what was unquestionably U.S. territory, and floating it north to their own sawmills. It was the beginning of the Paul Bunyan era and an industry that replaced the fur trade in the North Woods.

By 1870 the logging companies that had already depleted the stands of timber in Michigan and Wisconsin turned to Minnesota and within 30 years the lumbering town of Virginia, less than 100 miles south of the park, boasted the largest white-pine sawmill in the world. The 4000 lumbermen in the Minnesota woods in 1870 grew to 40,000 by 1900.

Logging was more than just the chief industry of the area—it was a way of life. The sight of a lumberjack in his checked mackinaw and spiked boots was a common one in towns throughout northern Minnesota. In the isolated lumber camps life was simple, full of hard work, and always intertwined with nature—though the effects on the land were devastating. Those who only heard or read about the life romanticized it. They saw not the scars of a clearcut, where not a single tree was left standing, but photos of a lumber camp dinner table covered with baked beans, meat, breads, potatoes, canned fruit, doughnuts, pies, and cakes. This latter image came to stand for the good life of a woodsman.

But what brought the country's attention to this remote area of northern Min-

Rainy Lake City in June, 1895 (Photo courtesy of Koochiching County Historical Society)

Logging camp in winter (Photo courtesy of Koochiching County Historical Society)

nesota was something dearer to human hearts than beaver pelts or towering white pines. In July of 1893, George W. Davis discovered traces of gold as he was panning some quartz on Little American Island near the southwestern shore of Rainy Lake. The news spread like wildfire and by 1894 the gold rush had produced several mines on nearby islands and the boom town of Rainy Lake City at the western end of the Kabetogama Peninsula off Black Bay.

The town was the classic overnight tent city, populated by miners and such colorful characters as "Patty the Bird," the village barfly, and "Gold Bug Jimmie." It was platted in May of that year and by July boasted a population of over 500. The town lasted six years, a remarkably long time considering the small amount of gold that was ever recovered. Over a dozen mines were recorded—a few on the American side and the majority on the Canadian side—with names such as Lucky Coon, Red Gut, Gold Harbor, Little Canada, and Alice A. By far the most profitable was Little American, which operated sporadically for seven years before closing permanently in 1901. The total amount of gold bullion recovered from the mine was worth less than $5000.

The Rainy Lake gold rush produced little in the way of immediate profits, but it did lead to a sudden influx of people into the area, who saw what other resources it had to offer. By the early 1900s Virginia & Rainy Lake Lumber Company, one of the largest in northern Minnesota, had completed a railroad line to International Falls and begun cutting white pine on the southern approaches to what is now Voyageurs National Park by 1907. A few years later the dams at the mouth of Rainy River, Kettle Falls, and Squirrel Falls—which separated Namakan and Rainy lakes—were completed, providing cheap power and more incentive for logging companies to begin cutting the northern side of the Kabetogama Peninsula.

Commercial fishing began in 1898 when a Canadian firm, Armstrong Fish Company, established a fishery on Rainy Lake and shipped its catch west by barge to Kenora on Lake of the Woods. The Canadian town became the center of Border Lakes fishing when companies based there began to cash in on the huge sturgeon runs. The fish often exceeded six feet in length and 250 pounds, but fishermen were more interested in the fish's eggs than in its flesh. The sturgeon roe was salted, kegged, and shipped to Germany to be processed as caviar.

When the caviar sandwich craze spread from Europe to the U.S., the companies found the profits good and the fishing easy. In 1895 Lake of the Woods companies processed four million pounds of sturgeon that produced 200,000 pounds of caviar. It was only a matter of years before the fish was wiped out and the companies moved to Voyageurs country to do the same to the runs in Rainy and Namakan lakes.

By 1914 the sturgeon industry was gone but commercial fishing was still profitable. More than 50 fishermen worked the area that is now Voyageurs National park, netting walleye, northern pike, whitefish, cisco, and burbot. Most of them sold their 70-pound iced catches to bidders at Kettle Falls, the hub of all this economic activity. Here, on the dock near the hotel, more than 5000 boxes of fish changed hands each season.

A blueberry industry had also begun in the area, and by the 1920s had become a competitive business. Local Indians would pick quarts of berries and trade them at a blueberry store on Dryweed Island in exchange for slips of paper. After

Early 1900s photo of women with Rainy lake sturgeon (Photo courtesy National Park Service)

Boom rings found throughout the park were used to haul logs to the hoist camps during early logging days.

the buying was over and the berries were safely stored, the pickers could redeem their slips for bread, canned goods, moonshine, or even cash.

As the depression of the 1930s settled over the country all the economic bustle in the area slowed to a crawl. Virginia & Rainy Lake Logging Company ended its operation in 1929 and the last tow of logs was sluiced through the Kettle Falls Dam in 1937.

People had arrived, they had profited, and now, for the most part, they were turning their attention elsewhere. What remained was the area's North Woods beauty—that could still be seen long after the loggers, miners, and fishermen were gone. Gradually this commodity became invaluable and a serious push for national park status began in the late 1960s. Congress authorized the park in 1971 and it was finally established in 1975 when state lands were deeded.

The healing had begun for Voyageurs National Park. The land is being reclaimed, the tote roads are slowly becoming lost in a growth of aspen and birch trees, the beaver has made a dramatic comeback. An attitude of taking and profiting has been replaced by a devotion to returning and preserving. People have come full circle in their regard for Voyageurs country: the beauty and adventure that lured the ancient voyageurs into the North Woods are once again the stimulus for those who visit the park today.

3 VOYAGEURS WILDLIFE

The rain began as a light drizzle in the morning and increased to a steady downpour by late afternoon. It drenched the lone kayaker paddling deep in Junction Bay and continued long after he dozed off in his damp sleeping bag. It didn't stop until more than 3 inches had fallen in less than 24 hours.

In nearby Net Lake the heavy rainfall was putting tremendous pressure on one point in particular—a 20-year-old beaver dam. The marvel of construction was 4 feet high and over 40 feet long and it dammed up the north end of the lake, allowing only a small stream to flow into Junction Bay.

The rain kept falling and the lake level rose until a crucial log broke and suddenly a 4-foot section of the dam gave away. A mountain of water rushed out of Net Lake and roared down the stream, flattening every sapling and plant that was growing within 6 feet of the banks. Then it was over and the only sound of water was the stream, now a mere dribble, and the rain that had turned to mist.

The kayaker crawled out of his tent the next morning and was stunned at the sight of Junction Bay: it was filled with debris, and logs, branches, and entire trees were floating past his campsite. He made his way into Net Lake—which was difficult, because the north end was no longer part of the lake but a shallow stream that meandered through mudflats to the main body of water.

But nothing prepared him for what he found in the lake. The water level had dropped 3 feet and all along the newly exposed shoreline were thousands of clams, stranded in the mud and easy pickings for whoever passed by. Seagulls were flocking to the area to feast on the delicacy, as were small mammals—pine martens, otters, or weasels—that devoured the clams and left neat little piles of shells. Even the kayaker was rewarded. The lake, now stirred up and reduced in size, provided some of the best fishing he had ever encountered. Almost every cast resulted in a perch or northern pike taking his lure and running with it.

The beavers had again drastically altered the environment, just as they had when they built the dam.

Fauna

Voyageurs National Park supports a wide variety of wildlife and flora, but no other animal or plant has shaped the history and the terrain as much as the beaver has. It was its unique fur that first brought western civilization into the Border Lakes region and opened up the voyageur's highway across Canada. Trapped to the edge of extinction by the mid-1800s, the beaver staged a remarkable recovery in the North Woods. In Voyageurs National Park today, biologists estimate that there are from two to three beavers per square mile, with colonies supporting up to six family members.

It is inevitable in Voyageurs that hikers and paddlers encounter at least one beaver. You are most likely to see only the head and a gentle wake as the beaver swims back and forth across a lake. What you will hear is the startling slap of its tail on the water—the animal's distinct warning to others that an intruder has arrived.

Deep water is the beaver's sanctuary. Large lakes are the animal's natural habitat, where it builds a home by burrowing into the banks. But inland the beaver creates its own environment by backing up streams as a safeguard against

Top, left: *Lady's slippers*. Top right: *Osprey nest*. Bottom: *Black bear*.

Beaver lodge over six feet high

enemies in the summer and a source of free-standing water under the ice during the winter. After impounding the water the beaver builds its distinct cone-shaped lodge that will house a mating pair, kits, and yearlings. Days are spent searching for food along the shore, storing willow and aspen trees under water for the winter, and maintaining the dam.

Dam construction begins with the cutting of trees. While the beaver's two upper teeth grip the trunk, the two lower ones actually gnaw at the wood with amazing speed. A beaver can drop a tree as thick as a man's thigh in 15 minutes. After creating a framework of trees, the beaver piles on mud, stones, and logs, for a structure that is considerably larger at its base than at the top.

The beaver, which can grow up to 40 inches in length and 60 pounds in weight, may be the largest rodent in North America and "nature's amazing engineer," but in the hearts and fears of park visitors, the animal takes a back seat to the black bear. An estimated 100 to 200 bears reside in Voyageurs National Park, ranging from a small cub following its mother to a lone male that tips the scales at over 300 pounds and is more than 6 feet tall when it stands on its hind legs.

Black bears will eat almost anything, though berries and tender roots are their primary food source. They are not social animals but are basically solitary, except for mothers with cubs. Survival is their most compelling instinct and bears will defend themselves, their food, and their young against any intruder, humans included.

Bears generally go out of their way to avoid people, but rare exceptions occur. Almost always the bear has been attracted into confrontations with visitors by dirty camps, remains of cleaned fish, or someone carelessly feeding them. Once a bear finds a campsite that is a source of easy food it becomes bolder and more destructive as it returns for more. Bears who fall into this habit eventually are trapped and relocated elsewhere in Minnesota.

Hikers who are following old logging roads through heavy brush or see signs of bears in the way of fresh scat, overturned rocks, or tracks in the mud should make noise to prevent surprise meetings. Keep bears out of campsites by suspending food and toothpaste at least 10 feet off the ground and between two trees at least 50 yards away, and fillet fish at an even greater distance. Keep equipment and dishes clean; and leave heavily scented items such as bacon and cheese at home.

If you encounter a bear unexpectedly, talk to the animal to let it know you are there and begin retreating slowly by walking backward. Never turn and run, which could prompt the bear to chase you. Often a charging bear is bluffing and veers off at the last second. Park rangers recommend throwing your hat or pack at an approaching bear, which may distract the animal long enough for you to back out of the situation.

One encounter most visitors cherish is the sight of two or three white-tailed deer bounding through a marsh area with white flags signaling their quick retreat. A count in 1984 estimated that the park contains three to four deer per square mile, and it is rare for a visitor to spend a week in the park and not spot one. Although they appear larger at a distance, even the biggest bucks rarely exceed 3.5 feet in height and 150 pounds. Deer paths are easy to recognize, especially through thick stands of aspen, because the animals eat the foliage along their way.

Encounters with a moose, on the other hand, are extremely rare and usually achieved only by hikers who are following tote roads deep into the heart of the Kabetogama Peninsula. The moose population in the park is currently extremely small due to early uncontrolled hunting. A 1983 winter census found only 38 in an area that could easily support 300 to 400. The number is so low that the loss of genetic diversity due to inbreeding may be preventing the moose's recovery.

Red neck grebe near its nest on Tom Cod Bay

The low number of moose and the declining number of white-tailed deer—due to the loss of the saplings they prefer as the forest matures—puts survival pressure on the wolves that live in the area. An estimated 30 to 35 wolves in six packs roam the park and the surrounding areas, with only one pack having most of its territory within Voyageurs' boundaries. Wolf sightings are extremely rare, even when cutting across the Kabetogama Peninsula, but you might spot the remains of a winter kill and occasional tracks. The most common sign of their presence is the howling backpackers sometimes hear at night.

Other mammals are more common and you'll have many more chances to see them. Among those frequently seen are the eastern chipmunk, which has five distinctive dark brown stripes; the red squirrel, known for its explosive, ratchet-like call that signals danger; and the stocky, short-legged woodchuck. You might also come across muskrat, showshoe hare, red fox, various species of bats, and the pine marten—which at one time was thought to be extinct.

The list of all the animals on land and in the water at the park is relatively brief, compared to the variety of birds that can be seen here. Nearly 240 different species of birds have been spotted in the area, making the park a birder's paradise. Even visitors who have never read a page of any field guide to birds

Remains of a winter wolf kill

Turkey vulture

should think about bringing some guidebook along. The numerous sightings pique the curiosity even of those visitors who have never studied the skies before.

The most famous avian resident of Voyageurs National Park is the bald eagle—the country's endangered symbol, which most people never see in its natural state. Often spotted resting on a dead snag or soaring high above the water, the adults are easy to recognize by their distinctive white heads and tails. Even an immature eagle, which doesn't develop its white field marks until its fourth year, can be identified by its large size. The bald eagle is one of the largest birds in North America, and in Voyageurs National Park is second only to the whistling swan, an occasional migrant to the area. An adult eagle's wingspan will often reach 6 to 8 feet. In 1984 biologists counted 14 breeding pairs in the park, along with an undetermined number of immature eagles.

Two other birds in the park are often mistaken for bald eagles, especially when soaring and only their undersides are visible. One is the turkey vulture, which is only three-quarters the size of the bald eagle. Like the eagle, the vulture is usually seen soaring or perched on dead trees. Its most distinctive field mark is the featherless red head of the adult, which is smaller than the eagle's head, and the two-tone blackish wings on its underside.

The osprey is the other bird often mistaken for a bald eagle. The confusion stems from its partial white head, but can be quickly resolved by checking for its broad black cheek patch, its most easily observed field mark. When soaring the bird can be identified by its white underside and distinctive black "wrist patches." When it spots its prey, it plunges feetfirst into the water.

There is also much interest by park visitors in the great blue heron, the lean, grayish-white bird that can reach a height of four feet. Fifteen of the 130 heron colonies in Minnesota are located in Voyageurs National Park. Colonies are usually located in dead ash trees standing in secluded beaver ponds or on pine-covered islands.

One of the most fascinating birds in the park is Minnesota's state bird, the common loon, whose distinct call has become a symbol of the North Woods. The unique position of its legs allows the loon to dive quickly and silently to depths of as much as 200 feet and remain underwater for a minute or more before resurfacing.

The loon is only one on a long list of waterfowl that have found a home in a park dominated by lakes. Paddlers are likely to see the mallard, common merganser, hooded merganser, common goldeneye, American widgeon, greater and lesser scaup, and ring-necked ducks in beaver ponds. Though they are only occasional visitors to the park, you may also see the red-necked grebe, bluewing teal, canvasback, bufflehead, and black duck.

In Rainy Lake, visitors have an opportunity to catch a glimpse of another rare aquatic species, the double-crested cormorant—immortalized by the Chinese, who put rings around their necks and used them to catch fish. Cormorants migrate to Rainy Lake every spring to nest and raise their young in large rookeries. Several are on the bare, rocky islands west of Fox Island, and are well worth a visit.

Those who take to the trails and tote roads will also see a wide variety of birds in the park. Hikers might be startled by a ruffled grouse darting in and out of the underbrush, making a harmless racket. Or they might hear the distinct tapping and then see several species of woodpeckers, including hairy woodpeckers, downy woodpeckers, and the common flicker. Redwing blackbirds clinging to tall stems of marsh grass are a common sight, as are blue and gray jays, the yellow warbler, and the broadwing hawk.

Flora

The most prevalent kind of tree in Voyageurs National Park is the aspen, with quaking aspen the most common species. Its dark green leaves are 2 to 3 inches long and can be recognized by their fine-toothed edge. The bark is smooth gray, or even yellowish green at times, and old aspen trees have a dark brown base. A large aspen may grow to 80 feet in height and a diameter of 20 inches.

A distant second in terms of numbers is the Norway pine or red pine. The tree, which reaches a height of 100 feet and a diameter of 40 inches is easy to recognize by its bark, which divides into large reddish plates as it matures. The dark green needles are 4 to 6 inches long and appear in clusters of two. Stands of red pine can create a spectacular sight as they naturally shed their lower branches and form a towering reddish forest of arrow-straight trunks.

White pine, the other sought-after prize of early loggers, is valued by campers today because its downed wood produces a quick, hot fire. The bark of older trees is deeply furrowed and grayish brown; that of younger trees will be smoother and greener in color. The white pine is easily distinguished by its needles, which occur in bundles of five, are three to five inches long, and appear bluish green on the upper surface and whitish beneath.

Other trees that grow in the park include white spruce in wet areas, black spruce in bogs and swamps, paper birch or canoe birch, balsam fir, white cedar along many lake shores, and jack pine.

Trees represent only a small part of Voyageurs National Park's flora, which is characterized by its abundance and great diversity, since over 300 plant species have been recorded. Most of them go unnoticed by visitors.

What catches the hiker's eye on the trail and in the marsh are the wildflowers. They begin blooming in May, some even before the last patches of snow have melted away, and continue far into the summer. The tote roads or logging trails may be wet and hard to follow at times, but they often lead to extensive patches of bright yellow marsh marigolds, deep purple wild iris, or the white wild calla.

Along drier ridges and grassy slopes visitors will encounter the reddish, sac-shaped eastern columbine, wild roses, or devil's paintbrush mingling with oxeye daisies to form a sea of oranges, whites, and yellows. Paddlers entering quiet streams and ponds may see a floating blanket of green lily pads, broken up by the flowers of the greater yellow lily, the tuberous, and the least white lily. A variety of orchids also grows within the park, most of them hard to spot. One of the most striking is the pink lady's slipper, with its large, sac-shaped flower, often found in the shade of moss-covered rocks.

If the flowers capture the hikers' admiration, then it is the wild berries that make their mouths water. Strawberries usually begin ripening in early July and blueberries in late July to early August, and there is a period of a week or so when both can be picked in one stroll along the trail to Cruiser Lake. Other juicy morsels available for those who search the foliage include dewberries, blackberries, wild raspberries, black huckleberries, thimbleberries, lowbush cranberries, juneberries, and wintergreen, whose green leaves and bright red fruit can be chewed or made into tea to obtain the refreshing mint taste.

Wild rice, the most famous plant of the Border Lakes region, grows in Voyageurs National Park but is rarely recognized by visitors. The grain, which often reaches heights of 5 to 8 feet by mid-August, can be identified by its wide, grassy leaves and clusters of seeds near the top of its stem. In the past wild rice grew throughout the park, but today only remnant beds can be found in sections of Cranberry Bay and Reuter Bay, while an occasional plant may be found in narrows between Crane and Sand Point lakes and along the Ash River.

Although most of the park is forested terrain, Voyageurs does support a wide range of bogs, marshes, and conifer swamps. These wetlands are the home of some very interesting plant communities—even if most hikers make a special effort to keep their boots dry by avoiding them. Swamps are different from marshes in that they support shrubs and trees, including black spruce and tamarack. Marshes are wetter than swamps and include various grasses, sedges, and bulrushes—but no trees.

Bog areas—or peatlands as they are commonly called—are by far the oldest of the three forms of wetlands. Most began forming after the last glacier retreated, making them more than 10,000 years old, and are identified by the bouncy mat of green sphagnum moss that carpets them. The moss acts like a sponge in collecting water and keeping the wetland cool, even on the hottest day. Two of the most interesting plants in the park thrive in bogs. Both are carnivorous plants and are able to grow in the infertile ground of a bog by consuming insects. The largest of the two is the pitcher plant, whose leaves form tubes that collect water and entice flies to land inside. The other is the sundew, which grows close to the ground.

4 NORTH WOODS FISHING

Tired of walleye, three Chicago fishermen asked a local if he knew of a good bass lake in Voyageurs National Park. Boat across Kabetogama Lake, he told them, to the Locator Lake trailhead. The lake was a "short hop" inland, he added, where there was a rowboat stashed among the trees. They could use that to reach Quill Lake for some of the best bass fishing around.

The eager fishermen crossed Kabetogama Lake early the next morning and turned into a narrow bay for the trailhead. But their craft never reached the dock. The water was shallow in May and they were forced to walk the remaining 100 yards through swamp mud so thick and viscous it almost sucked their waders off at each step.

Nor was the trail the "short hop" they were expecting. Rather, it was a 1.6-mile route that seemed more like 6 as they hauled their poles, nets, and tackle boxes over three steep ridges. Just as they reached the inland lake and were pulling the heavy rowboat into the water, two kayakers passed through. The bass fishing in Quill Lake was excellent, they said, but to get there you had to paddle through two lakes, climb over three beaver dams, and carry your boat across a 0.25-mile portage.

The kayakers took to the trail carrying their 35-pound boats. The fishermen rowed about 200 yards into Locator Lake, stopped, and looked at each other. Suddenly trolling for walleyes sounded good.

The bass in Quill were safe for another day.

Finding the Isolated Lake

Sport fishermen had established themselves at Kabetogama Lake long before the National Park Service did. It was only a matter of time before motorboats and fishing poles became the park's symbolic coat of arms.

But Kabetogama is only one part of the park. Even on the opening day of walleye season, there will still be only a handful of hikers and canoeists struggling across the Kabetogama Peninsula. And if the buzzing of fishing boats dampens your wilderness spirit, all you have to do is hike 0.25 mile inland to find solitude. There the fishing can be just as rewarding on lakes you can call your own.

Kabetogama is renowned as some of the best walleye water in the nation, and the park's other large lakes also provide good action for the luminous-eyed fish as well as for northern pike, smallmouth bass, and yellow perch. But many of the 26 smaller inland lakes can offer table fare of the same delicacy and still provide paddlers their cherished solitude with nature. In this respect, canoeists and kayakers have one advantage over those fishermen who arrive with their bass boat, electric trolling motor, and depth finder. Paddlers have the choice of fishing the popular larger lakes or moving inland to test a secluded body of water.

Regardless of where you dip your line, the entire park is considered walleye country by the vast majority of anglers who arrive. Its most distinctive features are its large, roundish, glassy eyes. These large eyes are an indication that the fish is light sensitive and thus it provides anglers the most activity at low-light periods such as dawn and dusk. The walleye is not known for its magnificent leaps out of the water or even for putting up much of a fight when hooked. What it is known for is the delicate white fillets that it produces and its superb taste.

Lucky fisherman with a pair of bass (Photo courtesy of National Park Service)

The Minnesota Department of Resources reports that walleye accounts for two of every three fish caught in the park.

The best fishing occurs when the fish have just returned to their summer grounds but before the lake's food chain is at its peak. The time frame ranges anywhere from early June to early July, with the good fishing lasting from two to four weeks. The fish will be found in water 5 to 16 feet deep in an aquatic terrain with distinct characteristics. Walleye like hard bottoms, sand, gravel, or rubble, and areas with a broken topography that provides access to deep water. This leads fishermen to search out rocky reefs, gravel, or sandbars, or the waters off narrow points of land.

Many anglers turn to live bait, including minnows, leeches, and night crawlers. Some fishermen believe that minnows are more effective during spring and fall and that a tail-hooked leech or night crawler on a harness rig seems to work better later in the summer. A wide range of lures is also used, including diving plugs, 3- to 4-inch spoons, and number 3 and 4 spinners.

The so-called "lindy rig" is standard hardware in Voyageurs National Park. The time-tested method consists of a slip sinker, which allows the fish to grab the bait and run with it without any resistance. At the end of the line with the bait is a "floater," a short, shanked hook with a bright colored jig head of styrofoam

Leeches can be caught and used for walleye and bass fishing

or cork attached to it. This will keep the bait 6 to 10 inches off the bottom, where walleye are often suspended when there is an abundance of prey to feed on.

Walleye fishing lends itself well to paddlers who find it difficult to do an extensive amount of trolling. Although most anglers search for the fish by slowly trolling reefs, sandbars, or points, once they feel a strike or a nibble they turn to still fishing. Walleyes are found in schools and if one is caught it usually means more are down below. Canoeists or kayakers will also find worms and leeches easy bait to use and keep in the back country.

The northern pike is more widespread than the walleye, and can be caught in all four larger lakes and most of the inland ones. The "wolf" of the Border Lakes does not compare with the walleye when it comes to feasting on a day's catch, but it is famous for its fierce battles with anglers.

A northern pike could be lurking in almost any shallow bay, cove, or shoreline where weeds, fallen trees, or stumps supply cover for the prey they feed on. They like to hide themselves among shoreline weeds, watching and waiting for schools of minnows which they scoop up in their shovellike mouths. Often in the Voyageurs area a beaver dam will be blocking the outward flow at one end of the inland lakes, providing the pike with an excellent place to hide and strike.

Anglers have reported hooking pike on almost everything from artificial lures and live bait to a chicken neck dangling from an oversized hook. What works best, especially for paddlers on an extended trip, are spoons and spinners. Particular colors or shapes are not important as long as they are bright and supply good action through the water. Wire leaders are a necessity because the pike's sharp teeth can easily slice through nylon.

Northern pike prefer baits that move swiftly, and a briskly retrieved spoon or spinner improves the final results. Drift or paddle quietly into shallow areas and cast along the fringes of weed beds or submerged logs. Be alert long after the lure has fluttered past the intended cover: pike like to follow their prey before striking, and have stunned more than one angler by taking a lure a few feet from the side of a canoe.

The northern pike's lookalike, the muskellunge, is also known to thrive in two of the park's inland lakes, and anglers have claimed to land it in several others. The muskie's spawning and eating habits are similar to the pike's, and anglers find early summer and fall the most productive time to catch one. The major differences between the two are the muskie's larger size and the amount of patience required to land one. Trolling with large spoons, feathered spinners, and plugs is the method fishermen use to land one, but it requires a great deal of time and a sixth sense for understanding the muskie's character.

The best opportunities for muskie fishing in the park are in Shoepack Lake, once the source of eggs for the Minnesota Department of Natural Resources' artificial propagation program. The lake is isolated in the center of the Kabetogama Peninsula and getting a boat in requires a cross-country portage. Muskies have also been caught in Little Shoepack, the adjoining lake south of Shoepack.

Smallmouth bass have been hooked in every large lake of Voyageurs National Park and are found in Little Trout, Lucille, Mukooda, and O'Leary of the inland lakes. Its cousin, the largemouth bass, is just as widespread.

The best times to catch smallmouth are early summer, from mid-May through June, and again in autumn when there is a bite in the air. The fish like cool water and hard rubble or gravel bottoms. Early in the summer the bass can usually be found in shallow bays, coves, shorelines, and reefs of less than 8 feet of water or at the mouth of a stream.

Many other species of fish provide good action and excellent eating in Voyageurs and the surrounding area. Yellow perch are as widespread as northern pike and can be taken throughout the spring, summer, and fall on worms, leeches, or small spinners. Lake trout are present in Cruiser, Little Trout, and Mukooda, three lakes with deep, clear water.

Regardless of what kind of fish you are after, fishing in Voyageurs National Park, Kabetogama State Forest, or Superior National Forest requires a Minnesota license. The state offers a variety of licenses for nonresidents that are good for a day, a week, or the entire fishing season. Fishing on the other side of the international boundary in Rainy, Namakan, or Sand Point lakes requires an Ontario license. If you are planning to fish in Ontario you must check in with Canadian Customs before entering and purchase all your minnows in Canada.

5 GETTING TO AND AROUND VOYAGEURS

It's less than a 24-mile drive between Cusson on US 53 and the portage trail to Johnson Lake, but it is easy to turn the trip into an afternoon adventure, or even an all-day journey. The dirt road winds and climbs and bends and dips its way through the Kabetogama State Forest and then a section of the Superior National Forest. It's the kind of road that makes you creep around every bend in second gear, anticipating a handful of white-tailed deer feeding along the side. It lures you into stopping at inviting lakes, scenic wetlands, or the Pelican River—which parallels it for a short spell.

It was well past sunset by the time my truck bumped and rattled its way to the end of the road at the Johnson Lake Portage trail, too late to hike into the isolated lake. The next morning I was up early preparing for my portage, along with the bugs. They forced me to cook breakfast one-handed off the tailgate, using the other to keep them from landing in my pot of oatmeal.

I ate in my cab and was polishing off my first cup of coffee when suddenly my pots and pans began rattling behind me. A fabled northern Minnesota mosquito stealing my pot of oatmeal? I turned to see not the mythical bug, but a huge black bear with half its frame stuffed inside the cab over the back of my pick-up. It looked up and we stared at each other—our noses three feet apart, with only a sliding rear window between them.

The bear lost its appetite. It wriggled its way out of the cab, knocking over pots and a jug of water, then backed into my kayak on the ground and fell on its butt. It quickly regained its dignity and slowly made its way toward the lake trail.

When the bear saw me out of the truck and shooting pictures, it turned sideways and growled like a dog. Then it was my turn to retreat: the bear could have the portage trail that morning. I settled for inside the pick-up and a second cup of coffee.

Getting to Voyageurs

Voyageurs holds a special niche in the National Park System as the only water-dominated park. The lakes make up a third of the park and the majority of its boundaries are in water, not on land. Roads approach the park at four points, but to reach the heart of the wilderness you must take to the waterways, a link to Voyageurs' past.

Located along the Minnesota-Ontario border, Voyageurs is 12 miles east of International Falls, 300 miles north of the Twin Cities, and 163 miles northeast of Duluth. The Minnesota Highway Department estimates that 92 percent of the park's visitors arrive by way of US 53, which connects Duluth to International Falls—the general staging area for most trips into Voyageurs National Park and surrounding areas.

Four roads departing from US 53 provide access into the park's waterways. The first is 95 miles north of Duluth at the town of Orr, where County Road 23 heads east and joins County Road 24 at Buyck. The route passes through Kabetogama State Forest and then the western edge of the Superior National Forest before ending at the south shore of Crane Lake, an entry point into both Voyageurs National Park and the Boundary Waters Canoe Area. The 25-mile trip from Orr to Crane Lake is a scenic one that winds past three lakes, the portage to Kjostad Lake, and the Vermilion River at Buyck.

Farther north is the Ash River Trail (County Road 129), which departs east and ends 11 miles later at Ash River, a cluster of resorts, docks, cabins, and the site of a pleasant little campground run by the Department of Natural Resources (DNR). Along the way, 7 miles from US 53, is the 4-mile one-lane spur to Kabetogama Narrows, the site of a VNP information station, a launching ramp, and a popular entry point to both Kabetogama and Namakan lakes. There are two primitive campsites within a 30-minute paddle of the ranger station and 21 more within a day's travel.

Three miles beyond the Ash River Trail turnoff on US 53 is County Road 122. The paved road heads north for the shore of Kabetogama Lake and then curves sharply to the west, where several side roads lead to the cluster of resorts on the lake. One of the spurs is a marked gravel road that ends at Chief Wooden Frog Campground, a DNR-maintained camping area with a launching ramp and a sandy cove for swimming. A mile before County Road 122 curves west, County Road 123 heads east and loops back to 122 after passing more resorts and the park's Kabetogama Lake Visitor Center along the lake shore.

US 53 continues toward International Falls and on the outskirts of the city passes Voyageurs National Park headquarters, with visitors' information and displays, including a 25-foot birchbark canoe built in the tradition of those used in the fur trade. Eventually US 53 reaches the heart of this logging town and comes to the junction with State Highway 11. To the east Highway 11 winds 12 miles to Island View, which overlooks the northwest corner of the park. Island View is another cluster of resorts and cabins along the water, and provides a public boat ramp near the end of Highway 11. The NPS also has plans to open a visitor's center there in 1987.

Vehicles can be parked and left at any of the five public boat ramps located at Island View, Chief Wooden Frog Campground, Kabetogama Narrows, Ash River, or Crane Lake. There is a parking fee, however, for leaving your vehicle at the Crane Lake ramp.

Getting around Voyageurs

The roads end where you park your car. Once you have reached the edge of the park all travel in and around the area is by way of the four large lakes that dominate the park.

Other national parks have front country, the section easily accessible by cars, and back country, wilderness that is reached by hiking or paddling during the summer. In Voyageurs, the larger lakes are occasionally described as middle country. The large bodies of water are crossed by motorboats, houseboats, canoes, and even an occasional sailboat as their occupants head for a campsite, favorite fishing hole, or trailhead. Despite the ease of getting around the park, the wild nature of the larger lakes requires visitors to be cautious and well prepared with proper equipment and life vests while offering a degree of outdoor solitude. Hence, middle country.

To enjoy the Kabetogama Peninsula and other backcountry sections of the park you must first travel through the middle country, and for some visitors that presents complications. For those who arrive without a canoe but want to paddle the park's interior, rentals are available from several outfitters located in International Falls, Crane Lake, Ash River, Kabetogama, and Orr. Rentals include

Kayaker in Cranberry Creek

paddles, life vests, and styrofoam car-top carriers for hauling the canoes to an entry point. Some outfitters even offer drop-off and pick-up transportation for an additional cost. Contact park headquarters for a current list of outfitters in the area.

Runabouts with small outboard motors can also be rented from many of the resorts adjacent to the park, to be used for travel on the large lakes. Resorts around the park are divided into four regions, each with its own association that will provide a list of its members and the services they offer. Write to the associations for more information:

Kabetogama Lake
Kabetogama Lake Association
P.O. Box 80
Ray, MN 56669
Phone: (218) 875-2621

Rainy Lake
Chamber of Commerce
P.O. Box 169
International Falls, MN 56649
Phone: (218) 283-9400

Crane Lake
Crane Lake Commercial Club
Crane Lake, MN 55725
Phone: (218) 993-2346

Ash River
Ash River Commercial Club
Orr, MN 55771
Phone: (218) 374-3141

Finally, for those visitors who want nothing to do with canoes or small boats but who want to see the park or hike its trails, Voyageurs has two NPS concession-operated tour boats that run naturalist-led trips throughout the summer on the park's four large lakes. It is possible for hiking parties to contact the concessionaires directly to make arrangements for drop-off and pick-up at trailheads. Each provides transportation in a particular region of the park. Both offer group rates and charter trips:

Rainy Lake
Rainy Lake Cruises
Route 8, P.O. Box 303
International Falls, MN 56649
Phone: (218) 286-5470

Kabetogama, Namakan, and Sand Point Lakes
Voyageur National Park Pleasure Cruises
1116 1st Ave. East
International Falls, MN 56649
Phone: (218) 283-8264

Voyageurs' Ice Roads

Vehicle access into Voyageurs National Park during the winter is primarily by way of the ice roads. Beginning near the end of December, when the ice on the large lakes is thick enough, the park maintains a 7-mile ice road on Rainy Lake from Island View to Cranberry Bay. A second one, from Crane Lake north to Mukooda Lake and beyond, is unmaintained.

The roads consist of a 40-foot-wide strip that has been plowed right down to the ice. Standard vehicles can use the roads and maintain control without special equipment such as chains. The only requirements are for ice fishermen to drill holes well away from the road, as they could cause flooding, and for all travelers to carry out their trash.

The Rainy Lake ice road is particularly popular since it provides access to the Black Bay Ski Trail. Drive east from International Falls on State Highway 11 for 12 miles, almost to the tip of Dove Island. The ice road begins here and heads straight for 0.5 mile to the Black Bay entry point to the trail system. Skiers park their vehicles right on the ice.

Shortly before reaching the Black Bay access, the road splits off and heads north out of Black Bay Narrows and into Rainy Lake. It curves east again and comes to a junction with the Dove Bay access to the trail system. Parking is also possible on Dove Bay. The road continues east until it reaches the mouth of Cranberry Bay. Skiers or snowshoers planning an extended winter camping trip would be better off to have someone drive them to their departure point rather than leaving their vehicles on the ice for a lengthy period, where they might be endangered by a sudden warm spell.

6 SUMMER BACKCOUNTRY USE

On the island campsite in Quill Lake two campers sat alone studying the stillness of the water around them. It was like glass, reflecting in perfect images the towering pines that crowded the shoreline.

Everything was quiet and motionless when far off in the west they heard a rumble rolling toward them. It became louder and louder, touching only needles of trees at first then swaying the entire forest and rippling the lake surface. The hollow groan made one camper shiver and tug on her wool hat and the other pull out his jackknife and carve on a log in front of him:

"The wind cries."

And it howls and it rumbles and at times it whispers so softly that it moves only the hair on your head.

Voyageurs National Park offers vivid images to those who pass through, and one of them is the wind. It greets visitors when they arrive, it accompanies them throughout their stay, it is there when they take the last stroke of their journey. It is a friend of paddlers and hikers when it keeps the bugs away on a warm summer evening, or pushes their canoes gently across a lake to their next campsite.

But it will also chill them, weaving its way through their heaviest wool sweaters and making them snuggle deeper into their sleeping bags at night. The wind is the number one danger to kayakers and canoeists. It comes suddenly, with little warning, even on the nicest days—often in short, hard blasts that form whitecaps on the smallest inland lakes.

In Voyageurs country you hear the wind more than feel it. Before it sways the needles in the tallest pines, you will catch its cry in the distance. It can be an eerie sound at night as it runs between trees, or a distinct howl when you hear it as you are paddling across the middle of a lake. The rumble in the distance becomes a warning that sends paddlers scurrying for the first cove or protected harbor they see. They sit safely on the shore and watch this force whip and boil the water in front of them, and then leave as quickly as it came.

In some national parks the moose is the symbol of their wild nature. In others it is towering mountain peaks or the hump on the back of a grizzly bear. To many backpackers in Voyageurs it is the wind that reminds them they are in a wilderness; that they must defend themselves against its chill and listen to it with sensitive ears when they paddle. And at night it is the cry of the wind that plays on their minds and fills their dreams with the North Woods.

Exploring the Area

There are three ways to explore Voyageurs National Park (VNP) in the summer, each suited to a different type of camper or backpacker. For those with limited backcountry experience, those with families, and those with no desire to exert themselves on a hiking trail or portage, VNP offers a rare opportunity in motorboat camping. The use of runabouts with small outboard motors for travel from one primitive campsite to another is popular in the park and allows inexperienced campers the luxury of carrying more equipment than a backpacker would, while spending less time and energy moving camp than those on foot or paddling.

Motorboaters are confined to the large lakes, however, and to campsites

Brown Lake Campsite

where they can land safely. They must also share their environment with the rest of the visitors, from fishermen to houseboaters, who depend solely on these waterways. To find total isolation, or to achieve that "wilderness experience," you have to work and sweat a little by picking up the paddle or putting on the hiking boots. Only then will you reach the hidden corners of the large lakes or sneak off into the interior of the Kabetogama Peninsula.

Voyageurs is a young park, and at this point in its development hiking opportunities are limited. Hiking consists of the 32 miles of maintained trails in the park, the Ash River Falls Ski Trail in the Kabetogama State Forest, and the miles and miles of old logging trails called "tote roads" that crisscross both the park and the state forest.

Almost 21 miles of the park's maintained trails lie in the Cruiser Lake Trail system, which traverses the peninsula from Lost Bay on the south shore to Anderson Bay on the north shore. These trails are well marked, planked through most wet areas, and connect eight primitive campsites. Other maintained trails, such as Black Bay Ski Trail or the Ash River Falls Ski Trail in the Kabetogama State Forest, provide day hike opportunities, while short trails to Locator and Ryan lakes allow paddlers and motorboaters on the large lakes to enjoy the isolation of an interior campsite without portaging in a boat.

Shoepack Lake as seen from the old fire tower

Voyageurs also offers cross-country possibilities for experienced backpackers. Unlike many of the older and more regulated national parks, Voyageurs has few limitations on where you can hike or camp. Few backcountry users and even fewer restrictions attract a certain adventurous spirit. These are backpackers who enjoy following a less visible path, an old logging trail, or just a route from one lake to another. They seek to take on the challenge of the terrain by using their wits to reach some isolated lake, and then get much personal satisfaction when they come to its shore.

The park is well suited for them. Much of it, especially the peninsula, is crisscrossed by tote roads that are old winter trails built by loggers. Many are still marked on topographical maps and some are surprisingly wide, dry paths through the woods. Others have been reclaimed by aspen trees, flooded out by a beaver dam, or are an impassable bog or swamp. All present a backcountry challenge to those who like testing their map-reading and compass skills.

But the best way to explore Voyageurs' backcountry is by canoe or kayak. Unlike neighboring BWCA's network of small lakes, streams, and portages, Voyageurs is dominated by four large lakes that offer the paddler wide open water and myriad islands, coves, and bays. The Kabetogama Peninsula in the middle, and other areas such as Grassy Bay and the Canadian shoreline of Rainy Lake, allow backpackers to portage and paddle their way into isolated areas.

There are literally dozens of routes you could follow, but several established ones are favorites among canoeists and kayakers, mainly because they eliminate back tracking and pass through particularly scenic areas of the park.

SAND POINT–NAMAKAN LAKE LOOP: An easy three- to-five-day trip, 32 miles long, that begins in Crane Lake and includes one portage. The route heads north by way of King Williams Narrows into Sand Point Lake to Namakan Narrows. The scenic narrows leads into the southeast corner of Namakan Lake, where the numerous islands and campsites make it a favorite among paddlers. The route returns through Grassy Portage into Grassy Bay.

KABETOGAMA NARROWS–NAMAKAN LAKE LOOP: The 46-mile trip begins at the Kabetogama Narrows boat launch and drops into Sullivan Bay to make use of the 0.5-mile portage from Ash River to Moose Bay. From Moose Bay the route continues along the south shore of Namakan Lake, passing through such popular areas as Junction Bay and the many islands near the north end of Namakan Narrows. The loop is completed by paddling along the Canadian shore on the east and north side of Namakan before reentering the park and following the Kabetogama Peninsula to the narrows.

THE KABETOGAMA PENINSULA LOOP: To circumnavigate the peninsula requires a 75-mile paddle that includes crossing two portages. The route can be started from a number of put-ins and could include many side trips or day hikes into the peninsula or along the Canadian shoreline. Paddling time is six to eight days.

LOST BAY LOOP: A popular trip that combines paddling with hiking the Cruiser Lake Trail or with short portages into the southern inland lakes. Paddlers could begin at either Kabetogama Narrows or Ash River and then use the short portage from Lost Lake to Lost Bay. Many backpackers paddle from Ash River to Cruiser Lake trailhead dock and then hike to Cruiser Lake campsite their first night, spend the second day hiking to Anderson Bay and back to the campsite, and use their final day to return to their departure point.

RAINY LAKE LOOP: The 80-mile route departs east from Island View entry point and follows the Rainy Lake shoreline within Voyageurs National Park. Although not in this book because it's outside the park, the loop can be continued by cutting over to the Canadian shoreline at Oak Point Island. From here paddlers can swing north and follow the Canadian shore west to return through Brule Narrows. The trip requires six to nine days, depending on the number of side trips planned, along with a spare day to sit out possible rough weather on Rainy Lake.

CHAIN OF LAKES LOOP: This string of inland lakes is the best way to view the peninsula's interior. From Island View the 35-mile route follows a portion of Rainy Lake and then Cranberry Bay to enter the peninsula by way of a portage along Cranberry Creek into Locator Lake. The loop is completed with a portage south from Locator into Kabetogama Lake and a second one, Gold Portage, into Black Bay. Five to seven days would be needed to reach all four inland lakes, and the route would include seven portages.

THE PENINSULA TRAVERSE: It is possible to traverse the Kabetogama Peninsula by canoe or kayak, a 28-mile trip that is best done from Cranberry Bay to Lost Bay. The route should be undertaken only by experienced backpackers since it includes five portages along trails and two more cross-country portages, one of them a difficult 2-mile overland trip from Loiten Lake to Shoepack Lake.

THE EASTERN INLAND LAKES: A string of inland lakes in the northeast corner of the park provides another route across the Kabetogama Peninsula from Namakan to Rainy Lake. A 46-mile loop can be paddled beginning from Kabetogama Narrows, and using the portage route of Mica Bay–Beast Lake–Brown Lake–Peary Lake to reach Rainy. The loop is completed by paddling east on Rainy to the American Channel and reentering Namakan through the Kettle Falls Portage. The trip requires five to seven days.

Permits, Fees, and International Customs

Because Voyageurs National Park runs along the Canadian border, visitors must be aware of the international boundary and customs procedures for traveling from one country to the other. When entering Canadian waters, you must first pass through customs as must Canadians entering the park along one of the lakes. Boats and motors must also be registered upon entering Canada, and visitors who land on the Canadian side have to report back to U.S. Customs when they return.

The Canadian Customs office most convenient to Voyageurs is near the mouth of Portage Bay in Sand Point Lake, and U.S. Customs maintains a station at Crane Lake. There are also offices in International Falls and Fort Frances.

Keep in mind that you may not bring live bait into Canada and can use live bait only if it was purchased from an authorized Canadian dealer and you have a proper receipt. You also need an Ontario fishing license when fishing on the other side of the border. The Canadians have a nightly charge of $3 for those planning to camp on Crown Lands, which includes most of the shoreline across from Voyageurs on Sand Point, Namakan and Rainy lakes. The general store next to the Canadian Customs office in Sand Point Lake sells Crown Lands camping permits.

No fees, reservations, or permits are needed for entering or camping on Voyageurs National Park itself but all watercraft of any kind must be registered, either

Camping in the rain

in Minnesota or in its departure state. If your state is one of those that does not require registration of canoes or kayaks, such as Michigan or Wisconsin, you must register with the State of Minnesota before beginning a trip in Voyageurs, Kabetogama State Forest, or Superior National Forest. A three-year canoe license can be obtained for $7 in person at one of the Deputy Registrar's Offices located throughout the state, including Virginia and International Falls. Or you can send for the application by writing to:

> Department of Natural Resources License Center
> 625 North Robert St.
> St. Paul, MN 55101

Backcountry Needs

Voyageurs country demands the careful planning and proper equipment that any park or wilderness would. You should consider your route before compiling your equipment list. Those who intend to stay on the outside waters with few if any portages can afford to carry extra gear or luxury items. But if your intent is to cross the Kabetogama Peninsula, consider everything twice before packing it.

FOOTWEAR: If your only desire is to hike the Cruiser Lake Trail system, a pair of well-broken but sturdy hiking boots is in order, as many of the trails wind over rocky ridges that pound your ankles and the soles of your feet. But the leather boots are almost useless when canoeing the park or following most other trails and tote roads. Many canoeists use an old pair of tennis shoes to hop in and out of their boats, or 14-inch rubber boots that will keep your feet dry on most tote roads into the interior.

TENT: A 6- to 8-pound nylon tent is sufficient as long as it has two things: a rain fly over the ceiling and insect netting on the door and windows.

RAIN TARP: Many paddlers find a rain tarp handy, especially if their trip is taking place in late May through June, the rainiest period of the summer.

STOVE: From May 1 to November 30 campfires are permitted only in designated campsites and day-use areas and must be contained within fire rings provided by the NPS. Wood is plentiful in the park, but it is still strongly recommended that backpackers bring a small stove to cook on. Campfires are nice for tranquil thoughts and warm feet on a chilly evening, but leave the cooking to your stove.

CLOTHES: Regardless of what time of the summer you arrive, be prepared for cool, wet weather. Rain gear, both pants and jacket, should be in every backpack along with woolen mittens, hat, and extra wool socks. From early July through mid-August the weather can be quite pleasant, and backpackers should have shorts and light cotton shirts for the warmer days and a swimsuit near the top of their packs for a refreshing swim.

ROPE: The park lies in black bear country and it is necessary to take proper safety precautions, including suspending your food at night. Usually two pieces of rope at least 25 feet each will do, with one used to hang the food bag 10 feet off the ground and the other to pull it away from the trunk of the tree.

MAP AND COMPASS: All backpackers should have in their possession a map and compass and knowledge of their use.

CANOEING EQUIPMENT: An extra paddle is not only good insurance, but can also double as a handy prop for the corner of your rain tarp. Each canoeing party should also have one life jacket per person and a small repair kit of duct tape, fiberglass repair, and silicone rubber cement for fixing any unexpected cracks in a boat.

Portages and Beaver Dams

There is no shortcut to portaging a canoe or kayak through the back-country of Voyageurs. The best way is still the way that the voyageurs used 200 years ago—you flip the boat on your shoulders and you carry it over the trail, returning later for the rest of your gear. If your boat doesn't have a portage yoke, build one before you come or else you'll end up lashing one together with sticks and your life jacket.

In many ways, cross-country portaging is like cross-country travel or bushwhacking. You are going from point A to point B without the aid of a trail or signs. You are depending solely on your map and compass skills and the natural landmarks you are able to identify to guide you. And you must keep a clear head and a calm disposition at all times to avoid getting lost and panicky. The difference is that in cross-country portaging the routes are considerably shorter, but you have to hike them three to five times before you are done. That is the key and the challenge to this type of wilderness travel: you not only have to find the next lake or stream, but you have to return to your original departure point at least once or twice.

Such travel may sound difficult, as if you will end up crashing blindly through the woods with a canoe over your head, but it won't be if you come prepared and follow a simple system for marking a route. Before you leave home put together a "flag bag," a small sack to be worn on your hip, filled with bright orange plastic strips or flags 8 to 12 inches long. If your route is 0.5 mile to a mile long, 200 will not be too many; if you are attempting the 2-mile route between Loiten and Shoepack lakes you will want at least twice that many.

Some backpackers mark their route the first time through, while others wait until the first return for a chance to improve on it. It is important to place the flags on small trees and branches at eye level and in such a way that you will naturally focus on one after another. Dense woods or sharp curves in your line of travel require a larger number of flags than does open terrain.

The boat is carried over on the second trip to your destination point. The person who is carrying equipment should be out front searching for the next flag and moving the brush back. The partner with the canoe on his or her shoulders should have to worry only about carrying the boat and listening for commands. In this fashion little time is wasted searching for the route when hauling your heaviest piece of equipment, your canoe or kayak, across the portage.

Flags should always be removed your last time through and returned to your bag, whether this is your last cross-country portage or your first. Most likely they will only confuse future parties trying the same route, as well as diminishing the "deep woods challenge" of cross-country travel.

Portages are not the only obstacles paddlers will run into as they travel through the peninsula or other backcountry areas of the park. Sooner or later—and most likely several times before the trip is over—you will approach a beaver dam.

Going downstream over a dam is easier than going upstream because the flooded pond allows you to paddle the canoe parallel to the top of the structure. Pick out a good-sized log that is solidly lodged into the dam and then gently step

Kayaker pulling his boat over a beaver dam

out of your boat onto it. If you miss, or it breaks, your foot will slip into soft mud that the beaver plasters this side with to keep it watertight. Pull the boat over the crest of the dam and allow it to slide gently down along the logs on the other side.

Going upstream is much more difficult. This side is a mass of sticks and logs protruding from the center of the dam, which makes hauling a boat to the top difficult. Some dams are so large it's easier just to portage around them.

Backcountry Water

Some locals will tell you that they have drunk water straight from the large lakes all their lives and never experienced any problems, while many backpackers filter all the water they obtain from streams and lakes. The NPS's official position, however, is that all water within the park should be boiled before drinking it.

It is possible that any lake or stream in Voyageurs country could be contaminated by the microscopic organism *Giardia lamblia*. Water can either be boiled for one full minute to make it safe or run through a number of microporous filters on the market today that are specifically designed to remove *Giardia* along with other impurities.

The water in many inland lakes and ponds vary in color from light brown to dark brown or even black. This coloration is usually found in low-lying lakes and is caused by suspended decomposing material that drains in from nearby swamps or bogs. While these lake surfaces can create magnificent reflections on windless days, the water itself causes alarm among paddlers passing through who are depending on it for drinking purposes. It is best to carry a supply of water if you have any doubts about the next lake you are traveling to.

Insects

To say "insects are part of any wilderness experience, bring plenty of repellent" is not enough for Voyageurs National Park. In this place, insects are more than just a slap on the neck. Their variety of colors and forms is intriguing, at times their numbers are overwhelming, and their magnetic effect on fish is amazing.

One of the most spectacular sights in the park is the hatching of mayflies in late May. The insect, which exists as a larva on lake beds and then rises to the surface, has little interest in people during its short life. But on windless evenings it's an eerie scene when clouds of hundreds of them slowly move through the air, filling the park with a low, constant buzzing. On the smooth surfaces of the lakes fish can be seen feasting on the insects, some merely plucking them off the water, others rushing at the mayflies with a hard slap of their tail.

Unless you come in mid-May or after August, expect something to nibble on you. Mosquitoes and blackflies appear in late May and peak from mid-June to early July, deerflies from late July through August, and gnats on most windless nights in mid-summer. You will also encounter wood ticks when traveling through tall grass or heavy underbrush. They tend to attach themselves to your pants and then work their way to your skin. Tick bites are unpleasant, but usually not dangerous.

Every visitor should carry a bottle of insect repellent, but your best protection during the day is provided by appropriate clothing. Wear long-sleeved shirts and tuck your pants into your socks or boots to stop ticks from walking up your legs—their favorite route. Your wool knit hat, though it might be too warm on a sunny August afternoon, is the best protection against the attacks of deerflies, especially for men with bald spots. If possible choose light-colored clothing for the trip, as dark colors in the blue and green range tend to attract more insects than do other shades.

Your best protection at night is your tent netting, so check it carefully and repair any holes before you depart for your trip. It's even worse to be kept awake by insects than to cope with them during the day or at dusk. You will also find that the island campsites on the large lakes catch any breeze in the area, making them natural sanctuaries from the persistent pests.

Weather

The paddling season begins when the lakes clear of ice in the spring, generally around the end of April. The daytime temperatures at this time average the high 50s and at night the mid-30s. They will rise continually until they peak in late July, averaging in the high 70s during the day, with a few afternoons breaking 80 degrees. By August they are dropping steadily again and by mid-September the daytime temperature averages 64 degrees and the nighttime 40. In October the highs range from the low 40s to the mid-50s and the lows from the

Eastern tiger swallowtail butterfly

upper 30s to below freezing. Ice on the lakes can be expected anytime after November 1.

Annual rainfall in Voyageurs country is 22 inches, with the rainiest season from June through early July. The rainfall is often accompanied by thunderstorms. Paddlers should be prepared for rain and lightning—perhaps in large doses—any time during the summer. And it's possible to encounter a snowstorm in May or September.

Thunderstorms are considered one of the greatest dangers to boaters on any body of water, especially the large lakes. The season for the dramatic displays of clouds, lightning, and thunder is during the warm weather of mid-June through early August. Visitors can usually spot the fronts moving over the wide expanses of lakes and often hear the thunder from a great distance. But electrical storms can form with little warning. Park rangers stress that *NO ONE SHOULD BE ON THE LAKES WHEN THERE IS THUNDER AND LIGHTNING IN THE AREA.*

Paddlers will quickly notice that winds, and thus wave action, seem to pick up suddenly around 10 or 11 A.M. then die down again after 5 P.M. Major crossing of the large lakes, or any paddle over 0.5-mile long in open water, should be scheduled in the early morning or late afternoon to make use of this natural buffer against high winds.

Those who arrive at International Falls and want extended forecasts for the duration of their trip can check the weather charts outside the NOAA Office in the terminal of the city's airport, located almost directly across from the VNP headquarters on US 53. You can also call a recorded weather message that runs 24 hours a day at 283-4615, or dial 162.55 MHZ on the weather band.

Visitor's Centers and Other Sources of Information

Voyageurs National Park has its headquarters on US 53 just south of International Falls and a visitor's center on Kabetogama Lake on County Road 123, 4 miles north of the US 53-CR 122 junction. At either one you can gather information, ask questions, buy maps, and look at displays that will give you a better understanding of the park. Park plans also call for the construction of a visitor's center at Island View across from Perry's Point in Black Bay to be completed and open to the public in 1987.

To request information or pamphlets in planning your trip write or call:

Voyageurs National Park
P.O. Box 50
International Falls, MN 56649
Phone: (218) 283-9821

A vast source of information and books on Voyageurs National Park and the surrounding area is the Lake States Interpretive Association (LSIA), a nonprofit organization that supports historic, scientific, and educational activities of the national park. LSIA sells topographical maps both for the park and for areas along the Canadian shoreline and in Kabetogama State Forest, along with numerous books that cover the history, anthropology, plants, and animals of the area.

Books can be purchased at any of the Voyageurs National Park visitor's centers, at the Superior National Forest visitor's center in Cook, or by writing to LSIA for its current catalog:

Lake States Interpretive Association
P.O. Box 672
International Falls, MN 56649

Preserving Voyageur Country

From fishermen and motorboat campers to paddlers and hikers, everyone must recognize the fragile and delicate nature of the park and its low tolerance for abuse. The wildlife can be tracked but must be left unmolested; the land can be loved but not stripped; the clear, cold water of the lakes, enjoyed but not polluted with waste.

At every primitive campsite within the park NPS rangers have posted these guidelines:

•Please keep your camp clean, pack out cans, bottles, and unburnable material—do not bury. Do not deposit cans, bottles, or garbage in pit toilets.

•Please build fires in the fire grates provided. It takes years for the vegetation to return where a campfire has been built on the ground.

•Please keep the lakes and streams clean by not washing your clothes and dishes in them. Soapy water adversely affects the plant and animal life in the park waters.

•Please do not cut boughs or trees. Dead or downed wood may be used for fires.

7 WINTER BACKCOUNTRY USE

Winter camper Steve Maass eyed the dim light that was filtering into his double sleeping bags, telling him that morning had arrived. Maass stirred, turned, and then managed to stick his nose out the small hole where the bags were gathered in by a drawstring. The cold air bit his nose. He yanked it back in and retreated deeper into his bags.

At 8 A.M. on February 16 it was −5° on the shores of Little Shoepack Lake in the middle of Kabetogama Peninsula. But Maass's bags, one inside the other, were lying on top of two closed-cell pads which in turn were wrapped in a tarp and set inside a snow trench. Inside his sleeping bags it was a cozy 72°. His nose said to stay put.

But it wasn't long before his bladder was indicating otherwise. He had to face the inevitable: it was time to get up. He wiggled and kicked to find the right items to make the departure from his winter cocoon a smooth one. Inside one bag or the other was his outer clothing, parka, a water bottle, his boots, boot liners, gloves, what was left of his middle-of-the-night gorp snack, and his camera—film often breaks in subzero temperatures.

He popped his head out and knew it was too late to turn back. He wasted little time in throwing on his clothes and boots and racing over to the snow mound designated as the latrine. He was as wild as they come, a madman charging through the snow with shirts untucked, parka unzipped, boot laces flying, Velcro straps flapping in the cold air.

He was so preoccupied with his task that it wasn't until his return that Maass

Winter camper (Steve Maass photo)

noticed the sunrise. It was just beginning along the east shoreline of the lake. First the horizon was painted in reds, followed by deep oranges, and finally the fiery orb broke through the pines and washed everything with a new set of colors. The two small islands in front of the camp seemed to rise with the changing light of early morning.

Instinctively Maass grabbed his camera and took a few pictures. Then he just enjoyed the spectacle, waiting for the sunlight to advance across the lake to the campsite on the west shore. A few pine siskins and chickadees were chirping their own awakening, but once they moved on, the silence returned. That is what an early winter morning promises most: silence and solitude, few people, no bugs, frozen waves under a deep layer of snow. The summers are beautiful in Voyageurs National Park, but Steve Maass says he will take the winters. The silence and the whiteness of the world around him has a purifying effect on him. It cleanses his soul, renews his spirit . . . and leads to a deep appreciation for a warm sleeping bag.

Winter Opportunities

In the summer, backpackers have to share the outside lakes with motorboaters. In the winter they encounter snowmobilers in certain sections of Voyageurs National Park. The motorized winter activity can take place along the outside lakes and on many trails into the Kabetogama Peninsula. But it concentrates on the routes to Cruiser Lake, the Chain of Lakes, and Mukooda Lake, where there is good ice fishing for lake trout. Most snowmobilers are local residents who enjoy their sport mainly on the weekends. Come the middle of the week and these lake trout havens are as quiet and deserted as the rest of the park.

Then there are some areas in the park that are disturbed in the winter only by a few pair of skis or showshoes—Grassy Bay and other points west of Sand Point Lake, for example, including the old Mukooda Ski Trail; Little Shoepack, Jorgens, and Quarter Line lakes, where numerous ridges prevent most snowmobilers from entering; and the developed ski trails of Black Bay and Ash River.

The eastern end of the park offers some of the best scenery and the most isolation, as there are very few snowmobile portages inland to Grassy Bay. An ice road, not maintained by the park service, connects Crane Lake with Sand Point Lake. Heading into this area of the park on showshoes or skis would be a challenging adventure, requiring at least four days to reach the deeper parts of Grassy Bay.

Routes into Little Shoepack, Jorgens, and Quarter Line lakes, or the Cruiser Lake Trail system, are best done with snowshoes. The terrain around these lakes is rugged and the trails were not designed with the nordic skier in mind. The same holds true for most tote roads within the park. The old logging trails, many of which are difficult to find in the winter, are usually covered with 2 or 3 feet of unbroken snow. Most are steep and have sharp turns, making them tough to slog through on a pair of skis.

Day skiing is best on the Ash River Recreational Trail in Kabetogama State Forest, which is groomed and tracked during the winter, or the Black Bay Ski Trail in Voyageurs National Park. Most overnight ski trips within the park take place on the Chain of Lakes. Locator Lake can be reached from Island View in one day by following a tote road—winter trail from the southwest corner of the Black Bay Ski Trail to the snowmobile route at the west end of Black Bay. From

Winter campsite on Little Shoepack Lake (Steve Maass photo)

here it is a 2.8-mile route due west along a tote road that ends at the east end of Locator Lake.

Skiers can also reach the snowmobile route by skiing along Black Bay, but should keep in mind that conditions on the large, outside lakes and bays are not always the best. If the snow is dry and powdery the open surface of the lakes will be highly irregular, with numerous snowdrifts giving them a sand dune effect. In these conditions, strong winds whipping across the lake surfaces often create whiteouts. Another problem you will encounter is the slush that forms between ice and snow, which makes for long days skiing and raises havoc with waxes.

Weather and Snow Conditions

Skiers and snowshoers can expect the first heavy snowfall that remains on the ground any time from mid to late November, and by Christmas they may be able to drive on the ice roads that lead into the park. The ice roads open from the last week in December to the middle of January and, depending on the winter, skiing usually lasts well into March—though the conditions might be crusty from a February thaw and refreeze.

Summer temperatures begin dropping in Voyageurs National Park in mid-August, and by the end of November the average highs are 24°F and the lows are 8°F. By mid-December the daytime temperatures are around 18°F and the nights are dropping to −1°F. Mid-January is the coldest part of winter, with the highs of 12°F and the lows dropping to −12°F (figures based on NOAA's 30-year average).

The park warms a bit by February, with days in the high teens to mid-20s F and nights at − 5°F. The highs in March hover around 30°F, the lows from 8° to 18°F.

The best time for an extended winter trip into the park is the first three weeks in February. During this period you can generally count on a good snow base and moderate temperatures, and you will have longer days than in December or January. Skiers will find the snow consistently cold, dry, and powdery in the first two months of the year, and can usually get away with only a small selection of hard waxes, such as green, special green, or polar. As the warmer temperatures and longer days of March soften the snow, skiers switch to blue, purple, and occasionally red wax.

Winter Needs and Equipment

The success of any winter outing in Voyageurs National Park begins with expedition planning. Whether it is a day ski along the Ash River Ski Trail or a four-day trek to the heart of the Kabetogama Peninsula, advance planning is your insurance against disasters. In the summer you can overlook a few items and still manage a rewarding experience, but the winters in northern Minnesota are rarely that forgiving.

If a trip requires a great deal of bushwhacking along poorly marked trails, showshoes are the preferred means of travel. They are much more maneuverable over fallen trees or through thick tag alder swamps than a pair of skis. Nordic skis are used on well-cut trails, lake surfaces, and some tote roads, where heavy underbrush is not a major concern.

BACKPACKS AND SLEDS: Soft-frame backpacks provide maximum freedom of movement and more comfort than those with a rigid outer frame. They are also more conducive to frequent spills on skis, but do have one drawback for winter camping: they tend to trap moisture along your back, something rigid frames reduce by providing ventilation space between your back and the pack.

For extended winter expeditions by ski or snowshoe, many backpackers use a sled to haul most of their gear and carry only a daypack with the essential items of extra clothing, water bottle, camera, and trail munch. A slightly modified child's plastic flat-bottomed sled works well for this method of travel.

SHELTERS: Most first-time winter travelers will carry a tent for their shelter. A small freestanding dome works best, and limits the number of stakes you need to keep it standing. Any tent that is used in the winter must have good ventilation to allow body moisture to escape, or else you'll be greeted in the morning with a snowfall from the ceiling.

Experienced backpackers can eliminate the extra weight of a tent by building a snow trench or snow cave. These alternative shelters, when built properly, provide more warmth and protection than most nylon tents. Snow is an excellent insulator, making it an ideal material for winter shelters because it retains body heat. There can easily be a difference of 40 degrees or more between the temperatures outside and those near the ceiling of a snow cave.

CLOTHING: It is best to follow what many backpackers term the "artichoke approach" when assembling your clothing for a winter expedition. The basic principle of layering, using two or more thinner layers as opposed to a single heavy one, should be applied to every part of the body.

Long underwear is essential. The best fabrics to choose are wool, the new pile types of polyproplyene, or even silk. Avoid cotton and the old-style heavy, insulated garments. Two layers should also be worn on the feet, with a heavier wool sock on the outside and a thinner light wool or silk sock on the inside. The same holds true for hands—a heavy pair of mittens with a wool liner is the most effective way of keeping them warm.

Light wool pants are ideal for midday activity, and you should include a heavier pair that can be slipped over the top for inactive periods at night. Light wool shirts and hooded parkas of 60/40 cotton-polyester blend, and perhaps an insulated vest, will keep you warm while skiing or snowshoeing. But for ending the day around the campfire you will need a heavy shirt, wool sweater, and a heavy down or dacron parka that is large enough to fit over all items previously mentioned.

FOOTWEAR: Feet are often the most troublesome part of the body to keep warm and dry. Snowshoers should have either insulated rubber "Korean" boots, waterproof shoepacks with a change of felt liners, or hiking boots with insulated overboots. Skiers will soon discover that the boots commonly sold with "ski packages" are usually too flimsy and poorly insulated for extended winter trips. Knee-high gaiters will also help immensely in keeping the bottom portions of your pants and the tops of your boots and socks dry.

FOOD: Because of the added requirement of keeping the body warm, winter travel and camping demand a high level of fuel in the form of food. Most people need between 3000 and 5000 calories per day and have to make a conscious effort to eat that much. The time of year is on your side, however, as the lower temperatures allow you to carry a wide variety of foods, including frozen meats, that you would never attempt in the summer. The worry of camp robbers is also gone, since bears are denning and pose no threat in the winter.

Winter demands a higher level of fats in the diet—they take longer to digest, thus delaying the gnawing sensation of hunger and chills caused by an empty stomach. One simple solution is to add butter to many dishes, including hot cereal, soups, gravies, cooked pasta, and even hot drinks.

The need to constantly refuel the body during strenuous winter activity cannot be overemphasized. Every daypack should include a good supply of gorp, candy, and nuts to munch on as you travel through the back country. Even when bedding down, many backers will take some gorp with them into the sleeping bag for a middle-of-the-night snack.

WATER: Because the air is drier and the body is exerting itself to stay warm, your water needs are often greater in the winter than in the summer. You can maintain a supply of unfrozen water by filling up a large plastic bottle with boiled water after each major meal. Or you can carry a smaller supply in a container placed in one of your inner pockets, where body heat will keep it from freezing. It is also important to take a filled water bottle into your sleeping bag at night. Not only does this keep your water from freezing, but also the water will be available for middle-of-the-night thirst, which is common in winter camping.

ODDS AND ENDS: The artichoke approach to clothing can also be applied to sleeping arrangements. Many backpackers find a two-bag system, with a medium-weight down bag for the liner and a medium-weight fiber bag on the outside, preferable to a single heavy sleeping bag designed for winter use. The two-bag system allows you to store clothing in the outer bag while keeping the inner one uncluttered for a better night's rest.

Winter campers should also plan on taking two closed-cell, full-length sleeping pads. The ground below will chill you faster than the sub-zero air above, and no part of your sleeping bag should be lying on bare snow during the night.

Hypothermia

Just hearing the word hypothermia is enough to send chills through most people. Though it's most often associated with winter, the condition can occur in any season when cold, wetness, wind, and exhaustion combine to prevent the body from maintaining its normal temperature. The first signs of hypothermia are uncontrollable shivering and the presence of goose bumps. This is followed by clumsiness, slurred speech, and loss of judgment. Eventually the victim may become badly disoriented, irrational, and unable to continue traveling. The final stages are unconsciousness and eventually death, if the body temperature drops below 78 degrees.

Most cases of hypothermia could have been avoided with better planning. Be responsible for your own clothing, and always carry enough warm items to cover an unexpected weather change or adverse situation on the trail. This is particularly true when it comes to protecting your head, hands, and feet, since the body loses heat first through its extremities. Up to 40 percent of your body heat can be lost through the head alone. Even on a day ski, there should always be an extra set of wool mittens, socks, and a hat in each skier's pack.

Avoid becoming overheated, which leads to excessive perspiration and dampness. Remove layers during intense periods of activity, such as skiing and snowshoeing. Eat and drink continually during winter expeditions. The body must have a high level of energy and fluid when working against the cold temperatures found in northern Minnesota during the winter. And finally, know your limits and avoid overextending yourself to the point of exhaustion.

If someone in your party exhibits the symptoms of hypothermia, build a fire immediately and move the victim out of the wind. Replace any damp clothing and give the person a steady flow of hot drinks and food, keeping in mind that carbohydrates take the least amount of time to produce heat. On extended winter trips, place the victim in a sleeping bag. If that isn't enough, remove your clothing and his and use your body heat to warm him.

(Opposite) Between War Club Lake and Quill Lake in the middle of the Kabetogama Peninsula

PART TWO

VOYAGEURS BY PADDLE

8 KABETOGAMA LAKE

At the junction of County Road 122 and US 53 there is a large statue of a walleye pike leaping out of the water. Its back is curved and its expression fierce. One after another, grinning visitors straddle the saddled fish, gripping the reins and waving to the camera from on top of the big one that got away.

It's no coincidence that this monument to a game fish overlooks the main entrance to Kabetogama Lake. To the Indians Kabetogama meant "lake above the other"; but to people today it means walleyes. The lake, long considered some of the best walleye water in Minnesota, attracts the largest number of visitors and certainly the most fishermen of any section of the park. They arrive full force in mid-May when the fishing season opens, and linger on well into autumn. Throughout the summer this body of water, the eighth largest inside Minnesota, is a scene of motorboats and fishing poles, minnow buckets and red and white bobbers.

The saving graces of Kabetogama, compared to more heavily used lakes farther south, are its size and the still moderate numbers of users that allow paddlers, motorboat campers, and fishermen to coexist on peaceful terms. The lake's 31 square miles include 78 miles of shoreline and 127 islands that fall within the park boundaries. Many visitors are content to use the lake during the day and return at night to one of the 30 resorts strung along the southwest shore. Those who stay to camp will find the lake quiet at night, with each party tucked away in its own island or shoreline campsite.

There are five entry points onto the lake: Chief Wooden Frog Campground, Kabetogama Lake Visitors' Center, Gappa's Landing, Kabetogama Narrows, and Ash River by way of Sullivan Bay, all supplying boat ramps and overnight parking. The NPS maintains 11 primitive campsites located on islands or along the shoreline. They are available on a first-come, first-served basis, and competition for them is often stiff, especially during the opening of walleye season and around the Fourth of July. Paddlers will pass numerous sandy strips or inviting islands that would serve well as overnight camping spots—minus the luxury of a table, fire ring, and pit toilet.

Although you could make a four- to six-day trip out of circling Kabetogama, for most paddlers the lake is a gateway to the park, a body of water to be crossed on the way to other more isolated areas. In this respect, few national parks have an entrance as beautiful as Kabetogama Lake.

SOUTH SHORE: CHIEF WOODEN FROG CAMPGROUND TO KABETOGAMA NARROWS

Distance: 14 miles
Portages: none
Paddling time: 1–2 days

Most first-time visitors to Voyageurs National Park (VNP) assume that Chief Wooden Frog Campground is part of the park, but the park boundaries actually begin at the water's edge. The campground is maintained and run by the Minnesota Department of Natural Resources (DNR), which charges a $5 nightly fee for each campsite.

Individual campsites back in the forest give privacy. A sandy cove and a boat

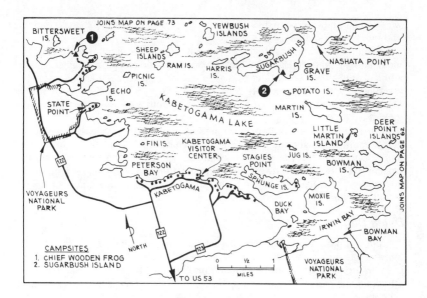

launch are only a short walk away. The campground includes tables, pit toilets, water, a trash receptacle, boat launch, public telephone, and an old stone hut where VNP naturalists give talks on a variety of topics throughout the summer. The campground is also within walking distance of a few resorts where you can purchase everything from a night in a soft bed to a bucket of minnows or a take-out pizza.

Those following the shoreline south will depart from the Wooden Frog boat launch and round a large point covered with resort cabins before passing between two nearby islands, the smaller Picnic Island 0.5 mile farther south and the larger Echo Island straight across from it to the west. Just beyond Echo along the shore is State Point, the long, distinctive peninsula named for the state forestry station once located there. Below the small cove it forms you will come to a rounded, unnamed peninsula with a number of resorts on its banks and then to Peterson Bay, where the shoreline curves in a more easterly direction.

The shoreline area from Peterson Bay to the channel formed by Sphunge Island 2.1 miles away is Kabetogama, a densely populated resort area. Motorboat activity is usually heavy here, with a constant stream of runabouts coming and going at the long line of docks along the shore. Paddlers should stay well off the lakeshore and travel cautiously, keeping an eye out for other boaters. The National Park Service has a well-developed boat harbor a little over a mile east of Peterson Bay. The Kabetogama Lake Visitor Center, offering books and topographical maps, is located just behind it.

Resorts and activity taper off dramatically once you pass Sphunge Island and enter the channel it forms with the mainland. The channel narrows down to Duck Bay which in turn opens up to the larger Irwin Bay. Both bays are surrounded by extensive marshlands that harbor a variety of waterfowl. Fishermen drift in occasionally, mainly in search of northern pike, but the conditions are poor for walleyes and motorboaters have to be cautious because of the shallow depths and numerous sandbars.

As you paddle southeast toward Irwin Bay, Moxie Island comes into view almost straight ahead. Between Moxie and the mainland is a smaller island situated at the lower end of Duck Bay and east of a small inlet. Farther east in Irwin Bay is a second narrow waterway, called Bowman Bay, which extends south almost 0.5 mile into the mainland. You can enter both waterways for close sightings of waterfowl.

Northeast from the mouth of Bowman Bay is the channel between Moxie Island's south shore and the mainland, followed by a small bay to the southeast and a long (unnamed) island straight ahead. Although marsh grass is slowly closing the narrow gap between this island and the mainland, it is still possible for paddlers to squeeze between them. Anything bigger than a canoe or kayak would get stuck.

Daley Bay

From the narrow gap between the island and the mainland you curve east into the channel formed by the main island of the Deer Point Islands and then pass through it to arrive at the wide mouth of Daley Bay. The 3.5-mile-long bay attracts a few motorboats in its upper half, but not many visitors in its deeper sections. You will find the mouth choppy whenever a northwest wind is blowing, but the rest of the waterway makes for a calm, interesting side trip.

When entering the bay, look to the southeast corner for a small stand of trees situated away from the rest. Located just west of those trees is the narrow gap

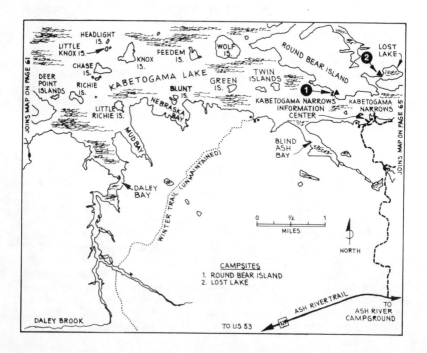

Canoers on Kabetogama Lake

into the second half of the bay. As you paddle through the small channel, to your left you will see fields of tall brown marsh grass swaying in the wind. Look carefully to see a variety of waterfowl, redwing blackbirds, or even great blue herons along the edge of the wetlands.

A little more than 0.5 mile from the gap, the bay narrows and makes a sharp U curve around a point covered with more marsh grass, then heads due south, continuing to narrow the farther inland it goes. You pass an old deteriorating dock and an ancient wooden boat on the west shore 0.25 mile beyond the sharp curve, then several arms draining from the marsh, most of them too shallow to paddle into.

It is a 2.5-mile paddle from the mouth of Daley Bay to where it splits into two navigable arms at its south end. You can paddle almost a mile down each one before the surrounding grassy shores and marsh areas close in on you. The arm due south eventually becomes Daley Brook, the small stream that can be seen while driving the Ash River Trail road from US 53.

The southeast arm cuts across an old winter trail still marked on early park maps and topographicals. To locate it paddle into the arm and look to the north shore. After a few strokes you'll pass a clearing where, among other things, you'll see an old red outhouse. The trail can be seen 20 yards beyond this and leads north to Kabetogama Lake. If you look at the south shore you'll see the section that leads back to the Ash River Trail. Although it is possible to hike the trail north to the lake, both segments are unmaintained, difficult to follow, and without inspiring scenery.

It is possible to camp deep in the bay, where you will have no visitors except the rich wildlife that thrives in the area. With all the nearby wetlands, however, in

June and July the bugs might prove to be overwhelming. You can find acceptable camping spots near the site of the old dock and in the grassy flats on the west bank of the southern arm.

It is 4.5 miles from the east side of the entrance to Daley Bay to the ranger station at Kabetogama Narrows. If a northwest wind is blowing the paddle will be quick and easy, with the breeze whipping you along the shoreline. But be careful rounding out of the bay and paddling to the channel formed by Little Richie Island and the mainland. This stretch, which includes the mouth of Mud Bay, can get choppy at times, with the swells perpendicular to your boat.

After passing through the Little Richie Island channel, you round a point and arrive at the mouth of Nebraska Bay. The east side of the bay, with its shield of Blunt Island, offers protective water to sit out strong winds or bad weather. If you don't have your maps close at hand you may be misled by the pair of islands in the mouth of Nebraska Bay into thinking that you have to paddle past two separate bays instead of one.

From Nebraska Bay the shoreline straightens out and is broken by only a half-dozen small coves. When you approach Twin Islands to the north, a mile after passing Blunt Island, you will see a large cove with a group of old buildings along the mainland. The old winter trail from Daley Bay terminates here and can be picked up by searching for it behind the large two-story faded red building in the center.

The next major inlet after the cove is Blind Ash Bay. A favorite among fishermen, the bay has a narrow opening and very protected water, making it a particularly good place to dip into when winds spring up. From Blind Ash Bay it is another mile east to the floating docks at the Kabetogama Narrows Information Station.

EAST END: LOST LAKE AND LOST BAY

Distance: 10 miles (round trip from Kabetogama Narrows to Cruiser Lake Trail)
Portages: 1
Longest portage: 0.25 mile
Paddling time: 1–2 days

Lost Lake, Long Slough, and Lost Bay make up the section of Kabetogama Lake that is a favorite among paddlers, fishermen, and motorboat campers alike. Lost Bay offers calm water and scenic shorelines and gives access to numerous lake portages and the southern end of the Cruiser Lake Trail. It was named by boaters who entered it thinking they were on their way to Namakan Lake.

From the floating docks in front of the Kabetogama Narrows Information Station, you can peer across the narrows and make out the point that forms the west side of the entrance to Lost Lake. It is almost a straight shot across the narrows, with a slight angle to the east. The paddle into the entrance is short, only 0.3 mile, but the narrows can be choppy when northwest winds and swells sweep across the lake and funnel into the gap between Kabetogama and Namakan lakes.

As you paddle into the narrow entrance the portage to Long Slough lies straight ahead and the route to the lake curves to the east.

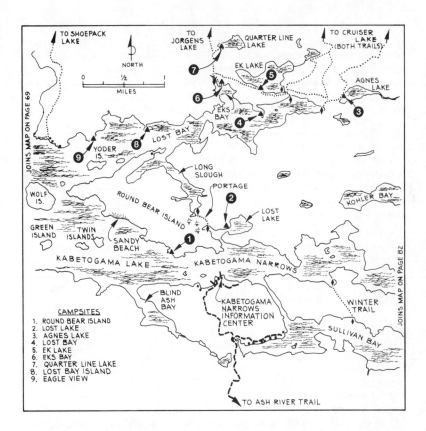

LOST LAKE CAMPSITE: You enter the lake through another narrow gap and then suddenly break out into a wide body of water. The VNP campsite is located inside, just north of the narrow opening, and is situated on a sloping slab of bare rock. A table, pit toilet, and fire ring are provided. Lost Lake and its campsite are a little haven away from the busy, choppy Kabetogama Narrows—combined with its easy access that makes it a very popular place to camp.

LOST LAKE–LONG SLOUGH PORTAGE (Rating—easy; distance—0.25 mile): Adjoining Lost Lake to the northwest is a small cove of weeds and marsh grass where every once in a while somebody lands a northern pike. The portage marker is hard to spot, half-hidden in the trees, but is located dead center on the north shore of the cove. The easiest way to find it is to look for the slice of channel in the marsh weeds where canoes have been pulled through.

The trail wanders through the trees for the first 20 yards and then breaks out along a ridge that provides a scenic view of the vast wetlands at the south end of Long Slough. It follows the ridge until it reaches navigable water. Both ends are marked, and the trail is level and usually dry.

As its name implies, Long Slough is a narrow inlet that runs over a mile in length from the portage north to where it empties into Lost Bay. The portage terminates near its southern end and you will need only a few strokes from the trail south to come to the vast marsh areas that you saw as you were hiking over from Lost Lake. The waterfowl are plentiful in this section, but you will have to view them from the outer edge of the marsh unless you climb out of your boat.

Paddling north a short distance you will come to a pair of small inlets, one on each side of the slough. The one to the east is a stream that is navigable for a short way until large fallen trees stop your progress. You might see some beaver activity here, even young kits playing along the muddy shore. Almost directly west of the mouth of this stream is the other small inlet, which has been dammed extensively by beavers.

A half-mile north of the inlets the slough opens up, with arms heading east and west. To the west the arm extends for 0.5 mile into a marsh area while the other one narrows down and empties into Lost Bay. From here you can shoot across Lost Bay, angling slightly west, and arrive at Lost Bay Island Campsite, one of four in the bay.

LOST BAY ISLAND CAMPSITE: The name is deceiving because the campsite is not on an island at all but is connected to the Kabetogama Peninsula by a thin strip of sandy beach. The campsite, which can best be seen from the west, provides a picnic table, fire ring, pit toilet, and space for several tents on a soft bed of pine needles. No matter where you stand you will be greeted with a clear view of the bay to the south.

Continue east along the north shore of Lost Bay, and in .25 mile you'll begin rounding a wide point. On the other side of the point is a large cove with an island situated at its opening. Once you paddle past the island you'll be heading straight for the narrow gap that Lost Bay flows through. Staying with the north shore, you'll flow through the gap, pass two coves and round two points, then find yourself drifting into Eks Bay.

Both the bay and the nearby Ek Lake are named after Ed Ek, a commercial fisherman who worked the area and at one time had a fish camp on the lake that bears his name. Two small inlets fork from the base of the bay, and the Eks Bay Campsite is on the spit of land between them. If you paddle up the western inlet you will arrive at the portage that winds 0.5 mile to Quarter Line Lake.

EKS BAY CAMPSITE: A scenic, comfortable campsite is located above the sandy shoreline at the tip of the small peninsula. It includes fire ring, table, open pit toilet, and space for numerous tents, including spots that overlook the western inlet. A path from the middle of the campsite departs along that inlet and joins the portage trail to Quarter Line Lake. From the campsite you can also reach the Cruiser Lake Trail to the east.

It is only a few strokes from the campsite back out to Lost Bay, which you reach after rounding the point that forms the Eks Bay mouth to the east. Heading east along the north shore you'll pass alongside a rocky islet, and from there will see a long, narrow peninsula. Lost Bay Campsite is at the southern tip of this peninsula.

LOST BAY CAMPSITE: Another gem in the line of VNP campsites, this one is surrounded on three sides by water and offers scenic views of both ends of Lost Bay. A fire ring and an open pit toilet are provided. You can sit here all day and study the scenery—if the bugs will allow it. A flat area between the towering pines is ideal for tents, and the tip of the peninsula, surrounded by large, smooth rocks, for soaking up the afternoon sun. What's unique about this campsite is that on one side you can watch the sunrise and on the other the sunset—both colorful shows reflected on the water.

The campsite's peninsula forms a narrow gap that leads into the east end of Lost Bay, a very scenic spot with a craggy shoreline and steep rock bluffs in the northeast corner. The area, especially near the small island and its surrounding weedbeds in the middle, is a favorite of fishermen. On windless evenings this section of Lost Bay is especially beautiful, since the narrow gap prevents even the slightest ripple from entering to disturb the stunning reflections of the shoreline on the water.

From here you can also pick up the portage to Ek Lake or the trailhead to the Cruiser Lake Trail. The portage is located on the north side halfway down, where there is a slight indentation in the shoreline. The 0.1-mile portage is marked, but the sign is difficult to spot. Not so for the trailhead to Cruiser Lake which is located almost at the very base of the bay. The sign is huge and you can spot it almost as soon as you pass Lost Bay Campsite.

If you arrive at a busy time and all the campsites on Lost Bay are occupied, keep in mind that there are three more a short walk inland. Quarter Line, Ek, Agnes Lake campsites are all about 0.5 mile from the shore along dry, level trails.

Heading west on the south shore from Lost Bay Campsite, you will soon pass a small bay that offers a sandy strip and some camping possibilities when it is

Trail bridge near Ek Lake

too late to go anywhere else. Cut across the mouth of the bay and head north-west up the large peninsula that forms one side of the narrow gap into the bay. On the east side of the peninsula is a high bluff of sheer rock—you can scramble up it for a good view of Lost Bay. If you are paddling close to the shore, you'll notice a boom ring embedded in the rock, one of the hundreds that can be seen along the lake shores. They were left by the lumber companies that logged the area in the 1920s.

Once you round the peninsula and head back through the gap it forms with the north side, you'll cross another small bay and then arrive at the narrow opening of Long Slough. The entrance is angled sharply to the northeast and partially blocked on the west by large boulders. You will have to pass the entrance almost completely and look over your shoulder before you can spot the mouth to the long inlet.

You should use Long Slough and its portage to Lost Lake for the return to Kabetogama Narrows if winds and waves are strong. The alternative to back-tracking is to paddle out of the bay and follow the outside shore of Round Bear Island back to the Narrows.

Just past the entrance of Long Slough is a small cove with a sandy strip occupied by an A-frame cabin. You are now following alongside Round Bear Island, which isn't really an island but is connected to the rest of Kabetogama Peninsula where the portage links Lost Lake with Long Slough. The name was originally Round Bar Island, after a saloon located on its shores, but a mapmaker's mistake changed it to Round Bear.

The shoreline curves to the southwest, broken by a small peninsula with a sandy neck, before you enter the channel formed by Yoder Island. Yoder is only a few strokes from the entrance of Lost Bay, across from the western tip of Round Bear Island. West of Round Bear Island is Wolf Island, with its high rocky bluffs, and to the northwest is another small island. The channel formed by Wolf Island and Round Bear Island is a favorite of fishermen trolling for walleye.

You will swing to the southeast through the Wolf Island channel and pass a shallow cove and a point forming its eastern side. Immediately after that is a second cove that features a nice stretch of sandy beach. This one is used often as a camping spot and even has a roughed-out fish-cleaning table along the beach. Round the curved peninsula that forms the southeastern side of this cove and you'll be headed for the southern tip of Round Bear Island.

Just before curving into the Kabetogama Narrows, you'll see a point with a pair of small inlets offering protection from the swells sweeping across Kabetogama Lake and sand to beach your boat. Just above the first inlet is the sign for Round Bear Island Campsite.

ROUND BEAR ISLAND CAMPSITE: This is a scenic campsite where you can sit at the table and view much of Kabetogama Lake. Sunsets on a clear evening are stunning, as the miles of lake surface turn shades of orange, silhouetting the many islands to the west. A fire ring and an open pit toilet are provided, along with a few choice spots to pitch a tent.

From the campsite you round the southern tip of Round Bear Island and flow into Kabetogama Narrows. It is a little over 0.5 mile to the floating docks of the Information Station. Paddlers should use caution when crossing the Narrows as the waterway is often choppy with the swells off Kabetogama Lake being funneled into it.

NORTH SHORE: LOST BAY TO SUCKER CREEK

Distance: 8.9 miles
Portages: none
Paddling time: 5–7 hours

The Kabetogama Peninsula forms the north shore of the lake and offers paddlers numerous opportunities to hike into its secluded interior along well-developed trails or old logging roads. There are three VNP campsites along this stretch and many other spots that offer camping possibilities.

The first campsite lies inside Lost Bay. From Lost Bay Island Campsite, heading west along the north shore, you will cross a wide bay marked by an island situated in the middle of its entrance. Eagle View Campsite is located on a point 0.75 mile to the west.

EAGLE VIEW CAMPSITE: The campsite is situated on the east side of the point, facing Lost Bay, and features a narrow slip ideal for beaching a boat. It includes table, fire ring, and open pit toilet. Many campers, however, land on the west side, where the point forms the east end of a sandy cove, and pitch their tents here beneath the stand of pines.

Paddle from the VNP campsite across the sandy cove it lies on to the head that forms the west side. As you round the squarish point you will see a group of privately owned cabins. Paddle past the last one and its dock, and beach your craft on the rocky shoreline. The Kabetogama Lake–Shoepack Lake Trail, which wanders 4.3 miles to the inland lake, begins above the shoreline, in the grassy flat. The trail is not marked and might take a little searching to find, but as it heads north it becomes a wide logging road (see chapter 13 for trail description).

Just a few strokes west of the trailhead is the mouth of a small stream flowing into Kabetogama Lake, followed by a narrow point. The point is the east end of a wide, shallow cove that features a long stretch of sandy beach for a possible

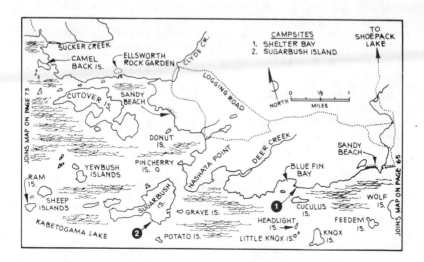

camping spot. Beyond the cove is another point, where a wilderness lodge still stands. With a few more strokes you'll be in the protective channel formed by Cuculus Island to the south.

Hug the shoreline and you will paddle straight into Blue Fin Bay, a scenic little area with calm water, the result of the small island that sits in the middle of its entrance. The name of the bay comes from the bluefins that people used to catch in its waters. In the late 1960s Boise Cascade Corporation, which then owned most of the peninsula, renamed it Shelter Bay and the campsite on its east side is still known as Shelter Bay Campsite.

SHELTER BAY CAMPSITE: You will spot the VNP campsite's dock and wooden staircase as you round the sharp point that forms the east end of Blue Fin Bay. Situated next to the sandy end of the bay, the campsite offers a table, fire ring, pit toilet, and plenty of space for tents on a bed of soft pine needles. Blue Fin is another popular walleye spot through much of the summer, so the campsite is usually occupied.

A narrow, sandy spit—a place where you could happily spend a sunny afternoon—makes up the west end of Blue Fin Bay. A quarter-mile west you will pass a small cove with a sandy strip on one side and then begin to curve northwest toward Nashata Point and the bay formed by Deer Creek. You will pass a half-dozen little inlets and coves before reaching the deep mouth of Deer Creek.

You can paddle amost a mile up Deer Creek, but the stream is slow-moving with a bottom of mud that sticks to your paddle like yesterday's oatmeal. Just after entering the creek from the back of the bay, you will pass an old green hut and a dock on the north side.

Both the bay and the waters that flow through the channel between Sugarbush Island and Nashata Point are popular walleye areas. At times it is possible to see as many as a dozen boats trolling this section. If a northwest wind is blowing, it will take a few hard strokes to paddle around Nashata Point and across the channel to the south side of Sugarbush Island—at one time the site of an Ojibway maple sugar camp.

Heading southwest along the shoreline of the large island, you'll spot a well-protected cove across from Grave Island, which lies to the east. After you pass Potato Island, which lies directly south of Sugarbush Island, the Sugarbush shoreline swings northwest. In a few strokes you will arrive at a small gravel strip at the east end of Sugarbush's large southern bay. The Sugarbush Island Campsite is located above the rocky shoreline among the trees.

SUGARBUSH ISLAND CAMPSITE: The campsite provides a table, fire ring, open pit toilet, and a good view of the island's long arm stretching out to the west. You can walk to the sandy strip of the bay a short distance north of the campsite or paddle at dusk to the tip of the arm, where there are always a few fishermen trolling for walleyes.

The reefs off Sugarbush's western arm are a popular trolling area, and fishermen occasionally camp on the eastern side of the long peninsula. But the bugs, especially wood ticks in the tall grass, make it a less than desirable spot for most campers. The bay has calm water, but at times, on the west side of the island, paddlers and motorboaters alike will have to battle waves and winds. Some protection is offered by the handful of islands that are scattered along the west

Author with his northern pike dinner

shore, allowing paddlers to leapfrog from one to the other when the lake is kicking up.

From the northern point of Sugarbush, it is a 0.5-mile paddle into the calm water of a small bay located on the west side of Nashata Point. A larger bay, located farther along the almost-mile-long point, has a sand and gravel beach next to an open grassy flat.

A logging camp existed here at one time, and some of its machinery can still be seen lying on the flat. An old tote road, used in the winter to haul sleds of logs out of the interior, swings by the shoreline of this bay. To the north the road curves into the nearby trees and quickly ascends a ridge. To the east the road cuts across a clearing, crosses a stream, and then swings to the southeast. Both segments can be followed to view the interior of the Kabetogama Peninsula. Eventually they lead to Clyde Creek, but the journey would be a challenging and wet one.

The western side of the bay is a short, round peninsula with Donut Island situated offshore. The peninsula also forms the east side of a long, sandy cove and two smaller ones. Once past these inlets you will be in the wide channel formed by Cutover Island to the west and the bay that shields the mouth of Clyde Creek to the east. Look for the privately owned cabin and dock in the back of the bay and paddle into the narrow inlet just east of them. The mouth of Clyde Creek is at the very end of the inlet.

Clyde Creek can be an interesting little side trip. The mouth is an impressive sight, with water tumbling down into the inlet between walls of sheer rock.

Ancient glacial activity is evident in a 4-foot-high boulder that sits balanced perfectly on a slab of bare rock near the entrance of the stream.

Just north of the boulder, on the same side of the stream, is a footpath that climbs 0.25 mile along Clyde Creek to a massive beaver dam and pond. Part of the original dam gave way and since has been repaired with an ingenious extension that fans out deeper into the creek. Sit for a spell and chances are good you will see a beaver go swimming by.

Directly across from Clyde Creek and the bay it flows into is Cutover Island, named after it was completely logged over one winter. Today second-growth trees cover the largest island in Kabetogama Lake and shield such wildlife as white-tailed deer and even black bears. The shoreline in the northwest corner is composed of high, rocky bluffs which can be climbed for good views of the surrounding lake.

The rest of the shoreline is broken up by almost a dozen coves and harbors. Many of them are on the east side and are composed of marsh grass and thick mud, making them difficult for paddlers to land in. Most of the summer, however, it is possible to paddle into the deepest cove in the southeast corner of the island and scramble across the narrow neck of land to the adjoining cove on the west side. There is a natural animal trail between the two and a variety of tracks can usually be spotted in the mud.

The west side is a dramatic change from the east—here the cove features brief stretches of sand, gravel beach, and even some grassy flats where a tent could be pitched. Head north along the shore and you will curve to what maps show as an island sitting just offshore of Cutover's middle arm. Most of the summer, however, a strip of grass and mud connects it to the rest of the island. On the south side of this "island" is perhaps the largest slope of rock in Kabetogama Lake, made smooth by a glacier 10,000 years ago.

Although the trees and underbrush are thick, you can cut across the middle arm of Cutover to reach the largest bay on the west side. The west shore beaches and coves of Cutover are a catchall for whatever the wind and waves may have washed ashore, and a little beachcombing will likely turn up a variety of items—everything from boat floats and old bottles to entire tree stumps, roots and all, and dozens of brightly colored fishing bobbers.

The channel between Cutover and the Kabetogama Peninsula offers not only calm water but favorable walleye conditions, attracting numerous fishermen throughout the summer. There is also another attraction along this natural waterway. As you follow the shoreline north from Clyde Creek, you will approach a small cove marked by a dock and a signpost topped by a birdhouse. This is the site of Ellsworth Rock Garden, built between 1944 and 1965 by Chicago contractor Jack Ellsworth for his own enjoyment. Today the garden is overgrown but still houses rock tables, 62 terraced flower beds, and statuary Ellsworth carved out of native rock. Trees screen it from being seen from the water.

After the rock garden the channel narrows considerably as it passes the bluffs on Cutover's northeast corner. A small island marks the place where the channel begins to open up to the northwest. This section can be choppy at times as waves and wind come sweeping in. Hug the shore and you will approach a head of land almost directly across from the western tip of Cutover. On the east side of the head, among the towering pines that block the winds, is an old camping spot. It's complete with some roughed-out log benches and a rock firepit where more than one party has waited out windy weather.

After rounding the head you will sweep into the channel formed by Camel Back Island and paddle through it to a pleasant little sandy point. This spit of land is the southern end of the wishbone cove that Sucker Creek empties into. North of the cove is an inlet with the remains of an old logging camp along its shore. There is also a tote road that departs from the ruins into the interior for 0.7 mile.

WEST END: SUCKER CREEK TO TOM COD BAY

Distance: 8.5 miles
Portages: none
Paddling time: 4–5 hours

Paddling northwest from the wishbone cove of Sucker Creek you will round a small point and then pass a shallow, sandy cove. Straight ahead a small island guards the north end of the cove, breaking up the surf and giving the harbor calm water and good camping possibilities. A second sandy cove appears 0.3 mile beyond the island on the south side of a small head. Round the head and you will spot the bare, smooth rock islet that marks the entrance of the bay where the Locator Lake trailhead for canoers is situated.

The entrance is a narrow slice in solid rock that opens up to the bay in the back. Canoers and kayakers rarely have problems in the bay, even in early summer or other periods of low water levels. Much of the bay is surrounded by marsh

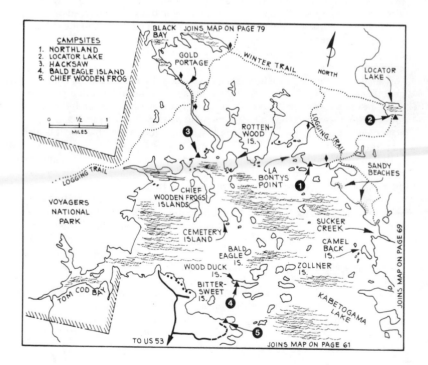

areas, and northern pike swimming into the shallow areas to spawn add interest in May.

The entrance of the bay marks where the Kabetogama shoreline begins to curve west to round the north end of the lake. Immediately west of the bay's narrow opening is a cove with a small area of grassy flats. Here at the main trailhead for the Locator Lake Trail is a dock and a large VNP sign. Follow the shoreline for another 0.25 mile and you will arrive at an even smaller cove where Northland Campsite is located.

NORTHLAND CAMPSITE: The campsite is actually situated on a rounded point of land from which you have three sides of Kabetogama Lake to view. From the campsite table you can study the length of the large lake and see dozens of islands scattered in all directions. Along with the table and fire ring, you have a covered pit toilet and a dock, but little level space for a tent. The dock is built high above the water, making it useless for low boats like canoes and kayaks, but paddlers can land their craft on a strip of sand in the back of the cove.

The numerous islands make the shoreline route from Northland Campsite to Hacksaw Campsite an easy 2.4-mile paddle through mostly protected water. The only crossing of open water is the large bay west of La Bontys Point, and even that can be eliminated by dipping into the two coves that form its backside. From Northland Campsite west you follow the shoreline and soon pass two islands to the south. The first has a small islet off its west end that is occasionally used as a camping spot. The second features an old log dock on its north shore.

You will cross a protected cove before reaching La Bontys Point. This is the place to land if any high winds or large swells build up on the large bay to the west. The crossing is a good 0.5 mile of open water, but can be avoided by taking the time to paddle deep into the east arm of the bay to circle behind the string of islands in the center. Hug the peninsula that divides the two coves, passing the old two-story frame house on its tip, as you head into the west arm. From this cove you return to the lake along the bay's west side.

A small cove running east to west marks the southwest corner of the bay. Just past its entrance are four islets. After you paddle through these the shoreline swings to the northwest, where you will reach a small point of land jutting out toward Rottenwood Island. Occasionally somebody will use this spot for a scenic campsite. Thanks to the winds that whip through the channel, it is also bug free.

Rottenwood, the large island straight ahead from the point, is named after an Indian family who lived on Kabetogama Lake. You can reach Hacksaw by paddling either north or south around Rottenwood. The southern route is shorter, but involves more open water. Paddle through the gap formed by Rottenwood and the small island just south of it. Pass the cabin on Rottenwood's southern tip and continue to hug the shore as it curves to the north. Another island will appear 0.25 mile off its west side. Follow a straight line from Rottenwood to the island to the mainland behind it. You should reach a small head; Hacksaw Bay appears as a very narrow inlet on its west side. The campsite is just west of the inlet.

The northern route to Hacksaw is slower but more protected. To avoid cutting across the channels between Rottenwood and the mainland, follow the shoreline north from the point that faces Rottenwood. You will pass numerous small coves, the mouth of the creek to Gold Portage, and an old deserted fishing camp before arriving at the head, 1.2 miles away.

Common mergansers swimming near the shore

Those who do cross over to Rottenwood should be careful not to get turned around by all the islands and channels around it. A common mistake is for paddlers to head straight from Rottenwood to the main Chief Wooden Frogs Island, thinking it is the mainland.

HACKSAW CAMPSITE: The campsite is located above a dock on the west shore of the small peninsula that gives it its name. It is surrounded by pines, and includes a table, fire ring, and open pit toilet. Nearby wetlands contribute to its heavy bug population through most of June and July.

Tom Cod Bay

Tom Cod Bay, a shallow inlet that runs southwest into an extensive marsh area, is an easy 2-mile paddle from either Hacksaw Campsite or Chief Wooden Frog Campground. Anglers like to fish around its mouth, just west of Sand Point Resort, but most avoid going into it because of the low water level and muddy bottom. Paddlers will find it an interesting side trip that can provide chances for waterfowl sightings and photography.

The entrance is wide, but almost immediately a head juts out from the south shore to form a narrow gap. The paddling gets more difficult from the gap past the marsh grass island straight ahead, and even those in empty canoes will find their boats scraping the bottom and mud clinging to their paddles. It is better to follow the island rather than the south shore for deeper water.

Once you are past the island the bay opens up, the water gets deeper, and the bird life prolific. You will probably spot a variety of waterfowl, including common and hooded mergansers. red-necked grebes, and mallards, along with great blue herons, an occasional eagle overhead, and numerous killdeers, common snipes, and spotted sandpipers running along the muddy shoreline. If you see a nest in the marsh grass, keep a distance from it. Otherwise you may chase off the parents and leave the eggs vulnerable to such predators as redwing blackbirds.

The bay narrows again and then opens up as the northern arm appears. You can paddle into that arm for a ways or head straight into the western arm until the water becomes so shallow even a flat-bottomed kayak can go no farther. Tom Cod Creek flows into the western arm along the south shore, but it is difficult to spot as its mouth is obscured by marsh grass.

CROSSING KABETOGAMA LAKE

Kabetogama Lake is a large body of water, 5.3 miles at its widest point, but it can be crossed in canoes or kayaks by following chains of islands at several different points. Although the islands reduce the stretches of open water encountered, paddlers still have to use caution traveling from one shore to another and should not attempt it when the winds are kicking up.

Sugarbush Island, near the north shore, is the start of two such crossings—one that ends at Chief Wooden Frog Campground and the other at Daley Bay. From the Sugarbush Island Campsite, paddle across the cove it lies on toward the tip of the island's western arm. At this point you will begin leapfrogging from one island to the next, beginning with the short hop from Sugarbush to Harris Island and ending at the DNR campground. Following Harris Island you are faced with a 0.4-mile paddle to Yewbush Islands and a 0.5-mile hop from there to Sheep Islands. Think twice before trying to save a few strokes by paddling the 0.7 mile of open water from Harris straight to Sheep Island.

On both Sheep and Ram islands there are sandy coves almost directly across from each other where you can stretch out if the sun is cooperating. Ram Island is followed by a 0.5-mile crossing to Picnic Island and from there it is only two short hops to Echo Island and then the mainland, just south of the campground.

If you head due south from Sugarbush Island Campsite, you can leapfrog to Potato Island, then Martin Island, Little Martin Island, and Deer Point Islands, just west of Daley Bay. The longest crossing is the 0.4-mile paddle from Little Martin to Deer Point, the others are all about 0.25 mile in length.

From Hacksaw Campsite you can follow a chain of islands that curves southeast right to Chief Wooden Frog Campground. The route begins with the short hop to Chief Wooden Frogs Island. Named after the Ojibway leader who lived in the Kabetogama Lake area, the island is almost a mile in length and has six coves along its east shore. Toward its south end on the east side is a round peninsula that features a grassy meadow and a protective cove on one side. In early summer it is a popular fishing camp for anglers after walleye and northern pike.

You can travel 0.25 mile south from Chief Wooden Frogs Island to Cemetery Island, the site of a Chippewa burial ground. There is a natural channel here, formed by the unnamed island that parallels Cemetery to the east. Your longest crossing is the one from the tip of this island to Bald Eagle Island—a 0.5-mile stretch of open water. An unnamed island lies 0.25 mile to the south of Bald Eagle, followed closely by Wood Duck Island, which has a VNP campsite on its western end.

WOOD DUCK ISLAND CAMPSITE: The campsite includes a table, fire ring, open pit toilet—and a lot of activity from the powerboats coming and going at the nearby resorts. From Wood Duck Island you cross the busy lane to Bittersweet Island and then on to the DNR campground.

KABETOGAMA LAKE TO ISLAND VIEW

Distance: 9 miles
Portages: 1
Longest portage: 0.2 miles
Paddling time: 5–7 hours

Backtrack to the old fish camp that sits on the small peninsula east of Hacksaw Campsite. This point of land and the larger peninsula northeast of it form one side of the mouth of the stream that connects Kabetogama Lake to Black Bay. For the next 1.2 miles the stream is wide and deep, occasionally attracting anglers to try their luck catching pike, perch, or even smallmouth bass. After 0.25 mile the first yellow sign, warning of rapids, appears. The stream follows a straight course after that.

After the second warning sign, the stream completes an S-curve, and you will hear the roar of the rapids before you see the white water. Local residents have been known to run the rapids in small rubber boats when the water level is high. You could even try it in an empty aluminum canoe if you don't mind a few extra dents—but that's for the thrill of white water on a hot sunny afternoon. If you're not looking for that, you should transport your boat and equipment by way of the short Gold Portage.

Right before the south end of the portage trail is an old logging trail labeled "winter trail" on topographical maps, that can be seen clearly on both sides of

Paddling the open stretches on Kabetogama Lake

the stream. To the north the trail leads toward the inlet off Black Bay, but would be a very wet, difficult hike during the summer.

GOLD PORTAGE (Rating—easy; distance—0.2 mile): The portage trail gets its name from the brief Rainy Lake Gold Rush in 1894. Then hordes of miners hiked over a longer version of it to what they thought were the riches that awaited them at Rainy Lake City on the shores of Black Bay. The trail turned out to be more enduring than either the stampede or the boom town.

At one time the trail ran almost the length of the stream on the west bank, but it recently was moved to the east side, where it allows paddlers to walk around the white water. The first half is level as it follows the high bank of the stream,

The rapids in the Gold Portage area

but the portage does climb a little before dropping down to its north end. The high banks at both ends of the trail make getting in and out of your boat a challenging and sometimes muddy affair.

Black Bay

From the north end of Gold Portage the stream resumes as a slow-moving, wide-water route free of any beaver obstruction. With only a few strokes, you come to the signs on both sides of the bank that mark the national park boundary. Gradually the high banks give way to wetlands and marsh areas, and from here through much of Black Bay the opportunities to sight waterfowl, great blue herons, eagles, and other birds are excellent.

The stream empties into a narrow inlet, marking the very southern end of Black Bay, but it will be close to another mile before you will finally be able to view the entire bay. Much of Black Bay, especially its southern half, is surrounded by marshes, making it an immense gathering place for birds and ducks. You should use caution when paddling through it, since the bay is wide and angled in such a way that northwest winds sweep down it, creating large swells and breaking waves.

Right before entering the open water of the bay you will pass an island to the north that marsh grasses are slowly connecting to the mainland. The island makes up one side of the inlet's entrance and features a cove that offers protection from high winds and a place to sit out rough conditions.

For those paddlers heading straight for Island View, the most direct route is to cross the 0.6-mile gap northwest to Skunk Island. The island, surrounded by islets, offers calm water on its east side. An arm on its west side is occasionally used as a camping spot. You can make a second crossing of 0.2 mile almost due north from Skunk Island toward a large "X" marker on the shore of Kabetogama Peninsula. From here you can work the shoreline as it curves from west to north by the time it passes Island View.

Along this shoreline you will pass numerous coves that can be dipped into for a breather if you are working against the wind. You will approach a large island

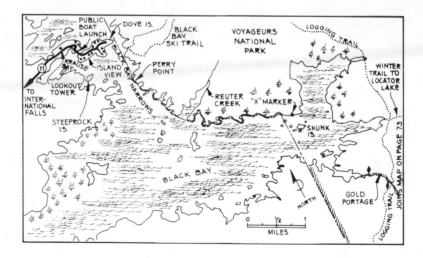

Pelicans taking off from Black Bay

1.7 miles after leaving Skunk Island. Stay on its eastern shore if your only intention at this point is returning to your car at Island View. Immediately following the island is the deep, narrow bay of Reuter Creek, marked on its north side by a stunning two-story cabin.

As you continue to curve north with the shore, you should be able to spot the Black Bay Lookout Tower, situated slightly northwest. After passing a handful of coves you will reach Black Bay Narrows, 1.2 miles from Reuter Creek. Glide past Perry Point, the point of land on the Kabetogama Peninsula that sticks out farthest to the west.

If you keep to the shoreline of the peninsula you will eventually reach the VNP sign that marks the entry point to the Black Bay Ski Trail, less than 0.5 mile north of Perry Point. The trail system is widely used during the winter by nordic skiers, but can also be hiked during the summer for a view of the peninsula's interior. Rainy Lake City, a boom town during the brief gold rush in 1894, was within 0.5 mile of the present trail.

From here it is a straight shot west past Steeprock Island into Krause Bay, where you paddle beneath the bridge to Dove Island to reach the public boat launch and parking lot. Those continuing into Rainy Lake would paddle north past the tip of Dove Island and follow the Kabetogama Peninsula shoreline as it curves to the east. Keep in mind that by 1987 there will be a VNP visitor's center and docking facilities across from Perry Point on the mainland.

9 NAMAKAN AND SAND POINT LAKES

Namakan and Sand Point lakes form the eastern edge of Voyageurs National Park and part of the international boundary between Canada and the United States. But the similarities between the two bodies of water end there. Sand Point is a small lake with eight campsites, two campgrounds, and a concentration of motorboat use that is second only to that on Kabetogama Lake.

Namakan is often the paddler's destination in Voyageurs National Park. The large lake offers a variety of scenery—everything from wide open stretches of water and myriad islands to steep-walled channels so narrow that it takes only three strokes to cross them. There are also 36 campsites, the majority on small, scenic islands, and opportunities to venture inland to isolated lakes and rivers.

There are no roads or boat ramps on the shores of Namakan, but the lake can be approached by the water from all directions. Visitors can reach the lake from the west by putting in at Kabetogama Narrows or Ash River; from the south by way of Crane Lake, Sand Point Lake, and Namakan Narrows; or from the north through Rainy Lake via the Kettle Falls portage. Paddlers can also enter the lake from the Boundary Waters Canoe Area or Quetico Provincial Park by following the rugged Namakan River, which empties into the lake's eastern shore.

NAMAKAN LAKE: ASH RIVER TO JUNCTION BAY

Distance: 7 miles (not including Junction Bay)
Portages: 1
Longest portage: 0.25 mile
Paddling time: 3–5 hours

There are two ways to enter Namakan Lake when putting in at the Ash River public boat launch. You can either avoid all portages by paddling Sullivan Bay and Kabetogama Narrows or you can carry your boat 0.25 mile from Ash River into Moose Bay. The paddle from Ash River to Moose Bay via Sullivan Bay is a 7.7-mile trip, adding almost another day of travel. Many paddlers use one route going and the other coming back to avoid any backtracking.

Departing from the boat launch, paddle northeast toward Sullivan Bay until you pass the brown cabins of the last resort on the Ash River. Look south and you will see the old railroad bed that serves as the portage trail, first following the river and then curving inland just before the mouth of a small stream.

ASH RIVER–MOOSE BAY PORTAGE (Rating—easy; distance—0.25 mile): The trail is part of the logging line that the Virginia & Rainy Lake Lumber Company built to haul logs out of Hoist Bay, the site of the company's short-lived hoist camp in the late 1920s. From Ash River the trail is a clear, straight, level path on which it is easy to envision the tracks and trains that used to run along it. After 0.25 mile the brush and trees give way to a long, narrow pond to the left and one of the narrow arms of Moose Bay to the right. Here paddlers can drop their boats into the arm and continue by water.

A few strokes and you quickly come to the bridge that crosses the inlet. Just beyond this is the junction where Moose River and the inlet come together and flow north for 0.25 mile to the south end of Moose Bay. The 1.6-mile-long bay flows northwest to Blind Indian Narrows, with the mainland forming its western shore and Williams Island much of its upper east side.

After a narrow gap formed by a round peninsula jutting out from the eastern shore, Moose Bay opens up and there are several islands straight ahead, the first a rather small islet less than 0.5 mile away. From this chunk of land you can see the channel to the east that is formed by the mainland to the south and Williams Island to the north. This is a shortcut into the middle of Hoist Bay.

Swing east into the channel, paddle a few strokes, and look toward the southwest corner of Williams Island for one of the two VNP campsites on the island.

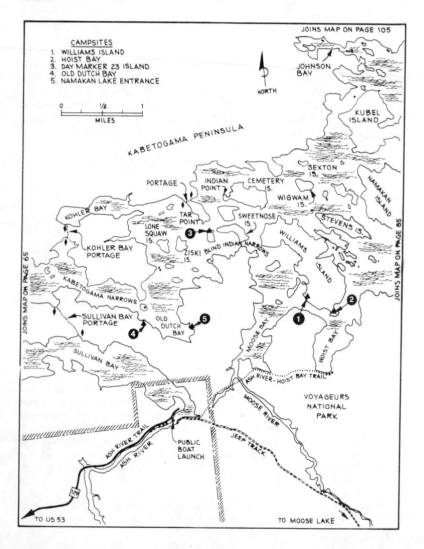

CAMPSITES
1. WILLIAMS ISLAND
2. HOIST BAY
3. DAY MARKER 23 ISLAND
4. OLD DUTCH BAY
5. NAMAKAN LAKE ENTRANCE

WILLIAMS ISLAND CAMPSITE: The campsite is located on a small point of land jutting out at the southwest corner of Williams Island. It features a table, fire ring, open pit toilet, and some pike fishing opportunities among the weed beds between the campsite and the long, narrow island just west of it.

The channel is 0.5 mile long and leads into the heart of Hoist Bay, where you can see a group of buildings to the south. This was the site of the old hoist camp and later served as a fishing camp, Youth Conservation Corps camp, and most recently housed biologists conducting research in the park. Paddle closer and you can still see the remains of the trestle where a steam jammer was used to load logs from the bay into waiting railroad cars during the heyday of the logging era.

On shore a trail that departs from behind the buildings and wanders west toward Moose River eventually reaches the east shore of Ash River (see chapter 14 for trail description). Part of the route follows the bed of the railroad line that Virginia & Rainy Lake Lumber Company laid in the 1920s to haul the logs out of Hoist Bay.

To the north, Hoist Bay is narrowed slightly by a head jutting out from the southern end of Williams Island. Paddle northwest around the peninsula to locate the second VNP campsite on the island.

HOIST BAY CAMPSITE: The campsite overlooks the entrance of Hoist Bay and is situated in a beautiful stand of red pine. The site includes a fire ring, open pit toilet, and a table where one can dine while looking at the bay and the south shore of Namakan Island. The shoreline near the campsite is composed of steep rock, requiring caution when you dock.

Across from the campsite, the shoreline of the mainland begins to curve northeast and then east toward the entrance of Junction Bay. You round one wide point, swing to the east, and in 0.5 mile arrive at a large cove with a sandy backside. The north side of this quiet cove is formed by a distinctively shaped peninsula that juts out into the lake at a 45-degree angle. Round this and you will be staring at a stretch of open water with Namakan Island bordering it to the north and the wide entrance of Junction Bay to the southeast.

It is a 0.5-mile paddle across open water from the peninsula north to Namakan Island, the largest island in the lake. The island has an interesting topography that includes rock bluffs along its south shore, a ridge that runs north-south across it, and an area of wetlands and beaver ponds in the middle. It is not unusual to spot deer or a black bear roaming the island.

Butting against the west end of Namakan Island is an L-shaped island with a cabin on it and just south of that a small island that anglers have turned into an unofficial fish camp, with a roughed-out cleaning table and stone fire ring. Along the south shore of Namakan Island are two VNP campsites. The first is located in the middle of the island, almost a straight paddle north after you round the distinctive peninsula along the mainland.

WEST NAMAKAN ISLAND CAMPSITE: Situated on a small cove, the campsite has an old dock and sandy strip where boats can beach. The table and fire ring sit on a bare rock point that catches any wind in the area; thus the bugs are kept away. An open pit toilet is situated in the back. Some high rock bluffs that line the small inlet can be climbed for an excellent view of Junction Bay.

Deer

EAST NAMAKAN ISLAND CAMPSITE: Almost a mile to the east, past two small coves and a large one extending 0.25 mile into Namakan Island, is a hammerhead peninsula. There is a small cove on each side of the peninsula; the western one is the site of the second VNP campsite.

The table, fire ring, and open pit toilet are set back into the trees in this campsite, making it more vulnerable to bugs than its counterpart to the west. The cove does have a sandy strip where you can beach your boat and a sandy bottom that makes it ideal for a midsummer swim when the temperatures soar toward the 80s.

Junction Bay

Paddlers who follow the shoreline east of the distinctively shaped peninsula on the mainland will pass two coves in the next mile, each with an island situated to the east. A sandbar that has filled in the gap between the first cove and its island, makes a comfortable camping spot. Once past the second cove you swing south, and from there will be able to see Hamilton Island in the middle of Junction Bay.

Junction Bay extends 2.3 miles in a southeast direction and has five campsites within it and four more just northeast of it. The area is a popular destination for many motorboat campers and anglers fishing for walleye, so it is not unusual for all the campsites to be occupied on weekends.

Just before you reach Hamilton Island you will pass the much smaller Postage Island that is often used as an unofficial camping spot. Two VNP campsites are located on Hamilton, both on its south shore.

HAMILTON ISLAND CAMPSITES: On the south end of the island between the two campsites is a cove with a gravel strip where you can beach your boat. Both sites have a table, fire ring, and open pit toilet. The one to the east overlooks Sheen Point and the large bay that it forms. The walleye fishing around Hamilton and Postage Island is good and it would be worth your time to do a little trolling near these islands.

Deeper into Junction Bay, on its eastern shore, is an old fishing resort where the owners still spend their summers. Almost directly across from it on the west shore is a small cove. Paddle into the cove to see and hear the waterfalls that the Johnson River creates as it empties into Junction Bay.

At one time it was common to paddle up the Johnson River into Little Johnson Lake, but today that would be possible only during extremely high water levels. Most of the time you will encounter your first logjam only 0.25 mile after portaging around the waterfalls. That is followed by more obstruction, shallow sections, and a few beaver dams.

But hiking along the river does provide an escape from the sometimes busy bay and provides a chance to spot a variety of wildlife, including deer, beaver,

CAMPSITES
1. WEST NAMAKAN ISLAND
2. EAST NAMAKAN ISLAND
3. HAMILTON ISLAND (2)
4. JUNCTION BAY
5. SHEEN POINT
6. McMANUS ISLAND (2)
7. WOLF PACK ISLANDS (3)
8. FOX ISLAND

and black bears. If you are wearing a pair of rubber boots it is an easy 0.5-mile trek up the river to a beautiful moss-covered gorge. The entire cross-country hike to Johnson Lake would be a very challenging trip, 2.4 miles one way.

At the southern end of the bay is the stream that flows from Net Lake and on the east side of it is the unmarked but well-worn portage to the lake. You could combine a portage into Net Lake with a short cross-country trek to isolated Tooth Lake just to the east of it.

Sheen Point marks the eastern side of the entrance to Junction Bay and forms the northern shore of a bay that lies directly across from Hamilton Island. A lone cabin lies half-hidden on the south shore. On the north shore two narrow peninsulas extending into the bay are occasionally used as camping spots.

JUNCTION BAY CAMPSITE: On the very western end of Sheen Point, a few strokes north of Hamilton Island, is a VNP campsite at the base of a long, narrow spit of land extending north. The site provides a table, fire ring, and open pit toilet.

NET AND TOOTH LAKES

Distance: 3.5 miles (round trip)
Portages: 2
Longest portage: 0.8 mile
Paddling time: 1 day

For those adventurous souls camping in Junction Bay, this can be a challenging single-day excursion that could result in a northern pike or perch dinner back at your campsite. Paddlers should undertake this journey with empty canoes or kayaks; since both lakes are bordered by either marshes or steep ridges, good camping spots are virtually nonexistent.

Once in Junction Bay, paddle to its south end, passing Johnson River Falls on the west shore. A small stream empties into the south end of the bay, and along its east bank is the unmarked but well-worn portage trail into Net Lake.

NET LAKE AND PORTAGE (Rating—easy; distance—0.2 mile): The portage trail, well established from years of use, runs along the east side of the stream, ascending slightly to the higher level of the lake. It ends up on the south side of a large beaver dam that in July of 1984 collapsed under the pressure of a heavy rainfall, lowering the water level of Net Lake by several feet. At that time the only way into the main body of the lake was to paddle—and sometimes pull—your boat through a muddy, shallow stream. If beavers rebuild the dam the previous water levels will return and paddlers will once more find it an easy trip into the lake.

Net Lake is 0.8 mile long and 0.25 mile wide at its south end, where it curves west into an extensive marsh area. The rest of the shoreline is made up of steep, wooded ridges that run from north to south. Although the maximum depth of the lake is only 12 feet, it provides good fishing for northern pike and perch.

TOOTH LAKE AND PORTAGE (Rating—difficult; distance—0.8 mile) Old-timers will tell you about a tote road that runs from Net Lake to Tooth Lake, and it is even shown on USGS topographicals, but locating it is almost impossible and trying to follow it even harder. That turns the trek between the two lakes into a cross-country hike—one that would be less difficult if you weren't trying to carry your boat through the thick brush and up the ridges.

In Net Lake there is a rounded point along the west shore where the lake begins to curve to the west. The old trail departed for Tooth Lake directly across from the tip of the point on the east side. Don't be dismayed if you can't find it. Just head due east to climb up and over a ridge to a large beaver pond on the other side.

Follow the pond around its south end to cross a dam and then continue halfway up its east side. To the east lies a low point between two ridges, which can be followed for the next 0.4 mile to reach the west shore of Tooth Lake. The lake, with an arm extending southeast, is 0.75 mile long, 0.25 mile wide, and has a maximum depth of 43 feet. It is worth the hike in for its solitude and excellent northern pike fishing.

NAMAKAN LAKE: JUNCTION BAY TO NAMAKAN NARROWS

Distance: 18.5 miles (including side bays)
Portages: 3
Longest portage: 0.4 mile
Paddling time: 5–7 hours

Return to the entrance of Junction Bay, paddle to the northern tip of the spit on the east side of the bay, and look to the east. McManus Island will lie to the north, Sheen Point to the south. The narrow gap straight ahead is deep enough only for canoes and kayaks.

SHEEN POINT CAMPSITE: Just south of the gap, on Sheen Point, is another VNP campsite. It is situated just inside a protective cove formed by the spit and includes a table, fire ring, and open pit toilet.

Long, narrow McManus Island lies just off Sheen Point and runs in a north-south direction. You can reach the east shore by paddling through the narrow gap between McManus and Sheen Point. Once there you will find a sandy cove toward the north end. The beach and sandy bottom make the cove a favorite swimming spot, and it is a short walk from here to the west shore. A narrow gap separates McManus from Sheen Island to the north, but it is slowly filling in and even canoes and kayaks might have problems paddling through it.

There are two VNP campgrounds on McManus Island. The first is located on its southern tip, a few strokes north of Sheen Point Campsite. The second is situated on the east shore just south of the sandy cove.

McMANUS ISLAND CAMPSITES: At the southern campsite the first thing you notice is the VNP sign at water level where there is a little beach to land your boat. The table, open pit toilet, and fire ring are situated high above the shore, with a good view of the mouth of Junction Bay and Namakan Island to the north. If there is a northwest breeze, bugs won't be a problem at this spot.

The other campsite is unmarked but is situated on the southern edge of the sandy cove. You will be able to see the table and fire ring from the water. An open pit toilet is also provided.

WOLF PACK ISLAND CAMPSITES: Due east of the gap between Sheen and

Fallen tree in Long Slough

McManus islands are the Wolf Pack Islands, the site of three more VNP campsites. On the west shore of the largest island are a gravel beach and a VNP sign for two of the campsites. The sign is visible as you cut across from the north end of McManus Island. Two paths from the beach lead in opposite directions to the island's campsites. To the left you climb an embankment and arrive at a campsite that includes a table, fire ring, open pit toilet, and a nice view of McManus and Sheen islands across the channel. To the right the path leads to a sandy strip on the south shore of the island where the table, fire ring, and open pit toilet of the other campsite are located.

Paddling along the south shore you will quickly come on the three other islands and the narrow gaps of water that separate them. On the west side of the largest one is the third Wolf Pack Islands campsite, with a table, fire ring, open pit toilet, and space for at least three good-size tents near water level.

FOX ISLAND CAMPSITE: Fox Island is located 0.3 mile northeast of the Wolf Pack Islands. It is marked by high bluffs along much of the west and south shores. There are two small coves on the north; the one farthest to the east is the location of a VNP campsite. The site overlooks Gold and Randolph islands to the north and the international boundary that runs between them. Campers will find a table, fire ring, open pit toilet, and a protective cove with a gravel strip for beaching boats.

From Fox Island you can paddle east between Randolph Island to the north and Jug Island to the south and for the first time view the wide open stretches of Namakan Lake. Up to this point Namakan has not appeared as a lake but rather a maze of islands and channels. To the east you will be able to see small Pike Island that lies in U.S. waters and the larger Gull Island across the border in Canadian waters. To the northeast is Canada's Sixdeer Island and to the south along the mainland is Randolph Bay.

There are a number of islands lying offshore at the west end of Randolph Bay, making it an ideal place to slip into if the waves start to kick up. Just east of the bay, 0.5 mile along the shore of Namakan Lake, are two small points harboring sandy coves. The second one is occasionally used as a camping spot.

For the next 0.75 mile the shoreline is an unbroken line of rocky coast until you begin to round a narrow spit angling off to the northeast. On the other side of the spit you will come to a superb beach in a quiet little cove. You will pass two more coves and then arrive at the narrow entrance to Deep Slough. The scenic bay extends almost a mile west and its waters are usually calm. At the mouth, on the south shore, is a spit that is connected to the mainland by a strip of sand. The east side of it forms a very beautiful camping spot, its sandy beach surrounded by rocky bluffs.

The bluffs are impressive and continue for a short way after you depart east from Deep Slough. It takes only a few strokes past them to arrive at a small bay where you will hear water tumbling. The falls are located in the back of the bay, and if there has been a recent rainfall, they will be worth viewing. There are three islands at the entrance of the bay, with canoe channels between them, and from here it is a 0.5-mile paddle to the gap between Juniper Island and the point extending north from the mainland. Once through, you can see the large bay where Grassy Portage is located to the south.

Hugging the western shore of the bay you'll pass a green cabin and then hear the tumbling of water. Pull up on the beach at this spot and cut across the narrow neck of land. Just a few steps over it is an incredibly large beaver dam and a pond filled with water lilies and accented by their bright yellow and white flowers. Sit a spell and chances are good that you'll spot some beaver activity.

You can paddle along the west shore for another mile before reaching the back of the bay, a marshy area in the summer where a snowmobile sign marks the northern end of Grassy Portage.

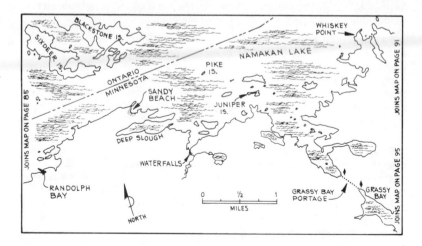

GRASSY BAY PORTAGE (Rating—difficult; distance—0.4 mile): Although marked as a snowmobile route for the winter, the portage is a key one for paddlers. It allows them to combine two favorite destinations, Grassy Bay and the islands around Namakan Narrows, into one trip without backtracking. The trail is basically a straight, level walk across to the northern end of Grassy Bay. What makes it difficult during the summer is its wetness. Hikers with rubber boots should be able to make it without getting their socks wet. After a heavy rainfall, however, a stream will be running the length of it, making it a little more difficult to keep your feet dry.

———————————

Following the east shore of the large bay north of Grassy Bay Portage, you will encounter a wide, slow-moving stream halfway up. The stream winds almost 0.5 mile east to a small lake surrounded by marsh grasses. A variety of waterfowl can frequently be sighted here.

Farther up the bay is a large cove, its entrance blocked by three islands. Once you round the point that forms its north shore, you will be back in Namakan Lake. The next 2 miles east the shoreline is broken up considerably by numerous coves, bays, and narrow inlets, each offering a hideaway from rough water and its own fishing opportunities. One point displays a red "Whiskey Point" sign and marks the west side of a cove in which the back is the narrow entrance to a 0.5-mile-long slough.

Just beyond the point that forms the east side of the cove is the channel southeast to Hammer Bay, marked with an island in the middle of its entrance. Paddle straight ahead and you will pass through a channel formed by a long, narrow island to the north and a much larger one to the south. At the east end of this short passage you can view Blind Pig Channel to the north and two of the 18 VNP campsites in this scattering of islands.

OWL ISLAND CAMPSITE: Straight ahead from the channel to the northeast is Owl Island, with a sign bearing its name, and the islet that parallels it to the north, a 0.3-mile paddle through open water. The VNP campsite is a scenic one—you can stand in the middle of the island and see water in all four directions. The open pit toilet is located in the middle, and there's a nice view of Pat Smith Island. The campsite also includes a table, fire ring, and gravel strip on the south shore for beaching a canoe or small runabout.

PAT SMITH ISLAND CAMPSITE: A 0.5-mile paddle through open water north of either the channel or Owl Island is another pair of small islands. The larger one is named Pat Smith after the commercial fisherman who, as the story goes, clung to the island whenever the lake kicked up. The VNP campsite features sweeping views, including a look at the international border just 0.3 mile to the north. It also provides a table, fire ring, open pit toilet. Like Owl Island it can be a windy spot, making it free of bugs much of the summer.

———————————

South of Owl Island are three large islands situated side by side, with two channels running between them. At its southern end the channel farthest to the west narrows down to a gap that only canoes and kayaks will be able to squeeze through. Straight across from it on a small island is an impressive rock cliff.

The island farthest to the east is Rusty Island, identified by a sign, which has a large cove and a VNP campsite on its north side. To the east of Rusty Island is the entrance to Hammer Bay.

RUSTY ISLAND CAMPSITE: The campsite actually sits on a high rock bank, but just east of it is a sandy strip where you can beach your boat. The site has a table, fire ring, open pit toilet, and like most of the islands in the area, catches even the slightest breeze to keep the bugs away.

RAINBOW ISLAND CAMPSITE: From Rusty Island Campsite no matter which way you follow the shoreline you will arrive in Hammer Bay, a 2-mile-long body of water that heads south then curves sharply to the west. Three islands are located in the middle of the upper half of Hammer Bay; the middle one is the site of Rainbow Island Campsite. The VNP sign sits on the north side of the island, but the only place to land your boat is on the south side, where a small section of mud breaks up the rocky shoreline. The site includes a table, fire ring, and open pit toilet.

The bay continues its southerly course for another 0.5 mile from Rainbow Island, then curves sharply to the west toward O'Leary Lake. It is a good 1-mile paddle from the turn to the portage trail. Along the way you will spot an old, abandoned cabin on the north shore.

O'LEARY LAKE PORTAGE (Rating—easy; distance—0.1 mile): The trail from the Hammer Bay side is unmarked but easy to spot. It is located in the southwest corner of the bay's backside, just to your left as you enter the mouth

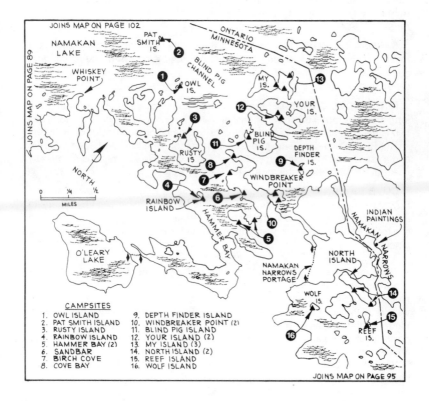

of a stream that flows out of the lake. A beaver dam stops you from going very far up the stream. The portage is short and dry as it gradually ascends to the higher level of the lake. The lakeside end of the trail is marked.

O'LEARY LAKE: This cold, deep lake is 1 mile long and over 0.5 mile wide at its southeastern end. Its clear water covers 190 acres and is 56 feet deep in the middle, making it a suitable habitat for lake trout. Anglers will also find good fishing for smallmouth bass as well as a few northern pike along the way. Much of the lake's shoreline is steep rock bluffs, but its northern end is marsh area. Camping spots are limited, but a small peninsula 0.3 mile north of the portage trail offers a few acceptable spots to pitch a tent.

As you return through Hammer Bay you'll see that the east shore from where the bay curves north is broken up by three deep coves. There are five VNP campsites scattered along this stretch, with the last two located due east of Rusty Island near the mouth of the bay.

HAMMER BAY CAMPSITES: After passing a hammerhead peninsula connected to the mainland by a narrow neck of land, you will pass the first cove that extends 0.5 mile east. From its entrance you can spot the VNP sign that marks a campsite on the north shore. The site, located in a growth of aspen and birch trees, has a table, fire ring, and two covered pit toilets. A path departs from the campsite and wanders north to the south shore of the next cove, where the other Hammer Bay Campsite is located. This one also features a dock, table, and fire ring.

SANDBAR CAMPSITE: Located on the north shore of the next cove is a pleasant campsite situated on a sandy point of land. Along with a table, fire ring, and open pit toilet the site also offers a fine swimming spot off the nearby sandbar.

BIRCH COVE CAMPSITE: From Sandbar Campsite you begin to round the long arm that forms most of the east shore of Hammer Bay. You will soon pass two islets. The second one, connected to the mainland by a rock bridge, is the site of Birch Cove Campsite. The site offers a table, fire ring, and open pit toilet and a sandy strip for beaching your boat. It is possible to scramble up the nearby islet for a good view of the mouth of Hammer Bay.

COVE BAY CAMPSITE: Just around the corner from the campsite is Cove Bay, marked by a sign, with a second cove hidden in the back. The VNP campsite is located on the north shore and its sign is visible as you cross the entrance. The site features a table, fire ring, and open pit toilet, all surrounded by towering red pines.

From the campsite you round the western end of the arm and come to the channel that it forms with Blind Pig Island to the north. Here you have access to nine more VNP campsites, considered the most scenic in the park by many visitors. If you head east you will pass through the channel and then reach Depth Finder Island Campsite, marked by a sign, 0.5 mile beyond it. If you follow the north shore of the arm you will pass through the channel and then drop south to arrive at two campsites, one on each side of Windbreaker Point.

North of the channel is Blind Pig Island, the first of three large islands in a line heading north. The others are My Island and Your Island.

Beach in front of My Island Campsite

DEPTH FINDER CAMPSITE: This small island campsite is the nearest one to Namakan Narrows. The site includes a table, fire ring, and open pit toilet, but there are not many places to land your boat along its rocky shoreline.

WINDBREAKER POINT CAMPSITES: Windbreaker Point, almost directly south of Depth Finder Island, has two campsites, one on its west side and one on the east. A path runs between them. The western one is a favorite, since it is situated in a stand of pines and has a sweeping view of the numerous islands north of it. The eastern campsite lies on the long inlet that gives access to the Namakan Narrows Portage. Each has a table, fire ring, and open pit toilet.

BLIND PIG ISLAND CAMPSITE: The site is located on the west shore of the island named during the days of prohibition. It is a scenic place to pitch a tent, since it lies on a point overlooking a small cove. Cliffs of craggy rock form much of its shoreline. Campers will find a table, fire ring, and open pit toilet. An interesting marsh area is a short walk beyond the sandy bar at the back of the cove.

YOUR ISLAND CAMPSITES: The island and its counterpart north of it picked up their names when the Canadians and Americans had a dispute as to who owned what. Day Marker 11 sits at the western end of Your Island, where two channels split off. The channel that heads almost due east follows Your Island's south shore and leads to the campsites, which lie next to each other on the west side of a small gravelly cove. Both have a table, fire ring, and pit toilet.

MY ISLAND CAMPSITES: The channel that heads north at Day Marker 11 will lead you along the south shore of My Island to the campsite at its southeast corner. A large log staircase is the most visible feature of the site. It leads to a table, fire ring, and pit toilet. Two other campsites are located on this island, both on the north shore overlooking Canadian waters. The second is situated in the deep cove in the middle of the island and features a stretch of sandy beach ideal for catching sun rays or swimming. Off to one side of the cove are the site's table, fire ring, and open pit toilet in a stand of pines. On the other side is a picturesque rock cliff.

The third campsite is a favorite among visitors and perhaps one of the most inviting places to camp in the park. It's located on a sandy spit sticking out of the northeast corner of the island. The west side of the spit is a beautiful beach. Among the pine trees in the middle of it are three sets of tables, fire rings, and pit toilets. The combination of the pine needles and sand is unbeatable for a deep sleep at night.

From the My Island Campsite you can paddle along the east shores of My, Your, and Blind Pig islands and then swing east toward Depth Finder Island. This is a major junction for paddlers. You can head east to enter Sand Point Lake through Namakan Narrows or continue on to follow the Canadian shoreline of Namakan Lake and eventually reenter the U.S. at Kettle Falls. Or you can head south, past Windbreaker Point into the narrow bay, to enter Sand Point Lake by way of the Namakan Narrows Portage.

NAMAKAN NARROWS PORTAGE (Rating—moderate; distance—0.4 mile): The trail is marked at both ends by snowmobile signs, but is surprisingly dry compared to many other winter portages in the park. The first 100 yards are level, then the trail descends the rest of the way to the bay south of Namakan Narrows. The portage can be used to avoid backtracking or to skip the busy waterway of Namakan Narrows entirely.

SAND POINT LAKE: NAMAKAN NARROWS TO HARRISON NARROWS, INCLUDING GRASSY BAY

Distance: 8 miles (not including Grassy Bay)
Portages: 3
Longest portage: 0.4 mile
Paddling time: 1 day

The Namakan Narrows, a picturesque passage of towering cliffs and bluffs, is a 1.1-mile paddle from the north end to Sand Point Lake. At its widest point, the Narrows is 0.25 mile from one side to the other, but in many spots it is less than 100 yards across. Paddlers should hug the shore and keep an eye out for motorboaters, who also use the waterway.

The most interesting sight in the Narrows is the Indian pictographs or paintings located on the sheer rock cliffs on the Canadian side. Many are faint and distorted from erosion and it would take a trained eye to spot them. But two can be easily recognized. From the north end of the Narrows, paddle 0.75 mile to a spit of land on the Canadian side extending out in a westerly direction. Paddle around that to the south and you will come to a sheer face of rock, perhaps the tallest one in the Narrows. As you begin to round it, look in the middle for a reddish moose 15 feet above the water. Paddle south around the corner on the other side of the rock wall and you'll see an orange man and some other figures 4 to 5 feet above the water.

From the pictographs it is only 0.3 mile to the south end of the Narrows, where you emerge at a junction with two other channels. The channel that heads west runs behind North Island but eventually becomes choked by marsh grass and

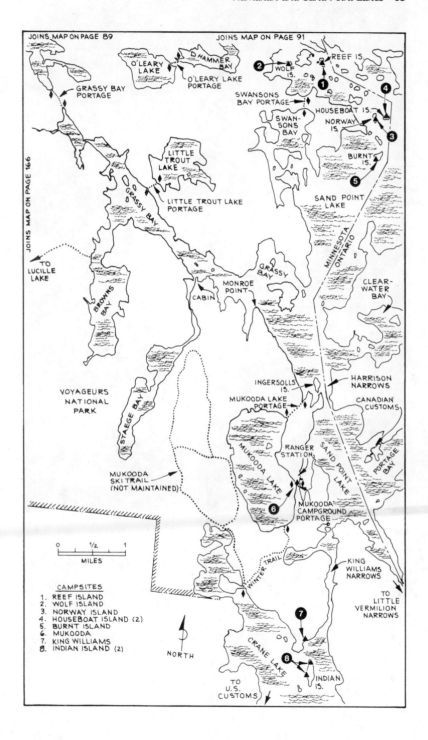

O'LEARY LAKE

D HAMMER BAY

O'LEARY LAKE PORTAGE

REEF IS.

WOLF IS.

GRASSY BAY PORTAGE

SWANSONS BAY PORTAGE

HOUSEBOAT IS.

SWAN-SONS BAY

NORWAY IS.

LITTLE TROUT LAKE

BURNT IS.

LITTLE TROUT LAKE PORTAGE

SAND POINT LAKE

GRASSY BAY

TO LUCILLE LAKE

GRASSY BAY

MONROE POINT

CLEAR-WATER BAY

CABIN

BROWNS BAY

MINNESOTA

ONTARIO

VOYAGEURS NATIONAL PARK

INGERSOLLS IS.

HARRISON NARROWS

MUKOODA LAKE PORTAGE

CANADIAN CUSTOMS

STAEGE BAY

RANGER STATION

SAND POINT LAKE

PORTAGE BAY

MUKOODA LAKE

MUKOODA SKI TRAIL (NOT MAINTAINED)

MUKOODA CAMPGROUND PORTAGE

WINTER TRAIL

KING WILLIAMS NARROWS

TO LITTLE VERMILION NARROWS

0   1/2   1
MILES

CAMPSITES
1. REEF ISLAND
2. WOLF ISLAND
3. NORWAY ISLAND
4. HOUSEBOAT ISLAND (2)
5. BURNT ISLAND
6. MUKOODA
7. KING WILLIAMS
8. INDIAN ISLAND (2)

NORTH

CRANE LAKE

INDIAN IS.

TO U.S. CUSTOMS

Canoeing through thick swamp grass (National Park Service photo)

impassable. Follow the other channel south and you will come to the island's south shore, where two VNP campsites are located.

Once you round North Island you will also be able to view much of the bay to the west that contains almost two dozen islands and islets, four VNP campsites, and the north end of the Swansons Bay portage.

NORTH ISLAND CAMPSITES: The first of the two campsites, a popular spot with a good view of Sand Point Lake and the many islands to the south, is located at the southeast end of the island. The site features a table, fire ring, and open pit toilet. Follow the south shore as it heads northwest and in a few strokes, toward the middle of North Island, you will come to the second campsite. The site, which provides a table, fire ring, and open pit toilet, overlooks the channel between two islands south of it. What it lacks is a suitable place to beach and secure your boat.

REEF ISLAND CAMPSITE: Another pleasant VNP campsite overlooking the international border, is located south of North Island. The site is on the southern tip of Reef Island and contains a table, fire ring, open pit toilet, and more sweeping views of Sand Point Lake.

WOLF ISLAND CAMPSITE: West of Reef Island Campsite is a small islet, a larger island, and then Wolf Island, located just south of the Namakan Narrows Portage. The campsite is situated on the west end and contains a table, fire ring, open pit toilet, and enough level ground for several tents.

SWANSONS BAY PORTAGE (Rating—easy; distance—0.3 mile): To the southeast of Wolf Island are three small islands, one of which has a cabin and a dock on it. Due south of these on the mainland you will see the snowmobile sign for the portage trail. The level area around the north end of the trail is occasionally used as a camping spot. The trail itself is a short, dry path that climbs gently for a short spell before descending to Swansons Bay, where it ends in a marsh area. Both ends are marked.

By combining this portage with the ones to Grassy Bay and around Namakan Narrows, paddlers can enjoy the deep, isolated bays of Sand Point Lake while staying away from the sometimes busy channels in the middle of the lake.

Following the mainland from the north end of Swansons Bay Portage, you will round a head and then hug the shoreline as it curves southeast out of the bay. You will pass a half-dozen islands and then round a point on the mainland that has a cabin and dock on it. Due east from the cabin is a pair of islands with three VNP campsites on them.

NORWAY ISLAND CAMPSITE: Norway Island is closest to the mainland, with the VNP campsite on its north shore. Along with a table, fire ring, and open pit toilet, the site contains enough level space for a number of tents. Nearby is a gravel strip suitable for beaching a boat.

HOUSEBOAT ISLAND CAMPSITES: Located on the north shore of Houseboat Island is a sandy cove with a campsite on each side. Each has a table, fire ring, and open pit toilet. One has a tent pad, since level space is limited in both. A short path cuts across from the cove to the marshy south side of the island.

Due south from Norway and Houseboat islands are a few islets; to the west of them is the tip of a mainland peninsula where a cabin and a dock are located. Once you pass the structures you will have a clear view of the upper half of Sand Point Lake. From here through to Crane Lake the number of motorboats on the water increases, along with the number of cabins along the shore. The only escape paddlers have from these intrusions is to travel deep into the many bays that break up the shoreline.

The large island to the southeast is Burnt Island, the site of a VNP campsite. After passing through the gap between the tip of the peninsula and the offshore islets, you will come to Burnt Island after a 0.3-mile stretch of open water that is often quite rough.

BURNT ISLAND CAMPSITE: The campsite sits on a bare rock slab near the south end of the island. It includes a table, fire ring, open pit toilet, and offers sweeping views of Sand Point Lake and its American and Canadian shorelines. A day marker sits on the island's south end.

From the tip of the peninsula the shoreline swings west, and more of Sand Point's open stretches of water come into view. The shoreline swings back to the south, where there is another cabin, then dips back into a small bay. Cut across that bay and you will arrive at the narrow mouth of Swansons Bay, a 1.2-mile paddle from Houseboat Island.

Swansons Bay is a long body of water that stretches 1.5 miles from one end to the other. In its mouth is a narrow island with a half-dozen cabins located on it. After passing the cabins, you paddle northwest through another gap and then arrive at the wide portion of the bay at its northern end. Straight ahead is one end of the Swansons Bay Portage Trail.

Much of the shoreline here is marsh area, as is the southern end of the bay. Many maps show a large island in the middle of the bay and to the south a narrow channel leading to the bay's entrance. But the gap on the south side of the "island" has been completely filled in and now requires a 20-yard portage to cross it.

Once you are back at the entrance, it is a 1.5-mile paddle past the cabins and bare granite bluffs just outside of Swansons Bay and along the unbroken shoreline that leads south to the entrance of Grassy Bay. As you are paddling the west shore from one bay to the next, much of the time you will be looking at a bare, smooth slab of rock that serves as a good place for an extended break, especially when the sun is warming it on late afternoons. Round that and you will see the point that marks the northern entrance to Grassy Bay.

Grassy Bay

Two islands hug the point and form a narrow gap in the north portion of Grassy Bay's entrance. Once you pass through the gap you will see a large bay to the north with an island and cabin situated in the middle of it. It is a 1-mile paddle to cross the wide mouth of the bay, at which point Grassy Bay begins to narrow down as it heads in a northwest direction. Hugging the north shore you will see another gap straight ahead, one side of which is formed by a rounded point.

It is a 1.2-mile paddle to the point. On the other side of the gap Grassy Bay opens up again, and straight ahead you will see three islands. Stay with the north shore and you will reach the Little Trout Lake Portage, located 0.25 mile before the shoreline curves toward one of the islands.

LITTLE TROUT LAKE PORTAGE (Rating—easy; distance—0.2 mile): An old, dilapidated dock is situated near the trail, and its logs can be used to pull your canoe or kayak up the shore. The trail is short and dry but begins with a rapid climb before leveling off for a few yards and then descending to the lake.

LITTLE TROUT LAKE: The roundish lake is 1 mile long from east to west and 0.75 mile wide from north to south. From the end of the portage trail you can view almost the entire lake except for its eastern arm where a private cabin is located. A short trail leads southeast along the shore from the portage, first passing a traditional camping spot and then dropping to the water to give shore fishermen an opportunity to try their luck. The 250-acre lake has a maximum depth of 95 feet and clear water where anglers will find both lake trout and smallmouth bass.

_____

Beyond the portage trail Grassy Bay turns into a picturesque scene of islands, craggy shoreline, and sheer cliffs over 100 feet high. A thin point of land extends from the mainland and forms a narrow gap with the island just offshore of it. There is good camping on both sides of the point; stone fire rings left behind by earlier campers are proof. Paddle through the gap and you will be awed by the bay's towering cliffs.

Beyond the islands Grassy Bay continues for another 1.6 miles in a northwest direction until it terminates with a narrow inlet where one end of Grassy Portage is located. Southwest of the islands is the entrance to Browns Bay. The mouth of the bay is a narrow gap formed by a round point jutting out from the west shore. Once you pass through the mouth and look to the west you will see the remains of a wooden dock. This was once part of an old state forest campsite that has since been dismantled. But while the pit toilet and fire ring are gone, the spot still offers a grassy area to pitch a tent.

A half-mile south is a rounded peninsula on the east side of Browns Bay; beyond it the bay opens up to more than 0.5 mile wide and extends south for another 1.3 miles. Across from the peninsula are a series of bare rock bluffs that slope toward the water. This is where hikers begin the route west to Lucille Lake (see chapter 14 for route description).

Departing from Browns Bay southeast along the south shore you will pass another old campsite 0.3 mile before the entrance of Staege Bay. It can be spotted by the table, which still remains. The mouth to Staege Bay is very narrow and is marked by a cabin and dock on one side. Paddlers and motorboaters have few problems traveling the 1.2 miles along the riverlike entrance of the bay to its wider section farther on. The 3-mile-long bay is an interesting side trip worth the extra paddling time. Its broken shoreline and towering bluffs along the east side provide scenery among the best in Grassy Bay.

Beyond the mouth to Staege Bay you will follow the south shore and cross two deep bays. The second is more than 0.5 mile deep and is formed by Monroe Point to the east. After rounding the point, where a cabin is located, you will have reentered Sand Point Lake.

SAND POINT LAKE: HARRISON NARROWS TO CRANE LAKE

Distance: 6 miles (to Indian Island)
Portages: 1
Longest portage: 0.1 mile
Paddling time: 2–3 hours

The shoreline from Monroe Point almost to Harrison Narrows is a straight, unbroken line where only a few points of land protrude. It takes only a few strokes to bring into view Ingersolls Island, which forms part of the narrows. After a 1.5-mile paddle, you will come to a small inlet with a cabin situated near the back. The inlet provides access to one end of the Mukooda Lake Portage, one of two trails into the beautiful, clear body of water.

MUKOODA LAKE PORTAGE (Rating—easy; distance—0.4 mile): The trail is level and surprisingly dry, considering it runs along a beaver pond most of the way, with the dam located toward the north end. Both ends are marked and from sign to sign it is 0.4 mile—although paddlers can put in before that to shorten the carry.

East of the inlet is the gap between Ingersolls Island and the mainland, from which paddlers can make their way into Harrison Narrows. From here it takes only a few strokes to enter the southern half of Sand Point Lake. Hug the west shore as it angles slightly southwest. After 1.2 miles you will pass the VNP ranger station and then arrive at the dock that marks one end of the second portage into Mukooda Lake.

MUKOODA CAMPGROUND PORTAGE (Rating—easy; distance—0.1 mile): The portage and campground are marked by a large VNP sign. The trail is an easy walk up a bare rock slab directly to the multiple-site campground on the lake shore. Easy except when it rains—then the rock turns slippery and paddlers must take care not to slip while carrying their boats.

MUKOODA LAKE AND CAMPGROUND: The campground has six tables and fire rings, two covered pit toilets, a water spigot, and ample room for dozens of tents. It also features a fine view of the lake and a hand pump that gushes some of the sweetest water in the park.

The 1.7-mile-long lake is 1 mile wide and 78 feet at its maximum depth. It's generally thought of as one of the most scenic lakes in the park and an angler's delight. Fishermen catch smallmouth bass, perch, northern pike, walleye, and an occasional lake trout. Follow the lake shore north of the campground and in 0.5 mile you will come to the largest island in the lake, a place where anglers congregate in the early mornings and evenings.

Almost due west from the campground are two smaller islands in the lake; the one to the south is occasionally used as a camping spot. Climb up the shore on the mainland west of the islands and you will find the old Mukooda Ski Trail. Though it is no longer maintained by the VNP, the trail still can be followed south to reach Crane Lake's most northern bay.

From the Mukooda Lake Portage, paddle north out of the bay where the trailhead and VNP ranger station are located. Canoes and kayaks can squeeze through the gap between the tip of the peninsula that forms the east side of the bay and the islet just north of it. Once through it you will be in the open water of Sand Point Lake again. Follow the outside shoreline of the peninsula south and in 0.3 mile you will round a bend in the land and see the opening of King Williams Narrows. To the southeast you should also be able to spot the entrance to Little Vermilion Narrows, the western gateway to the Boundary Waters Canoe Area.

It is another 0.75 mile south to the entrance of King Williams Narrows, a very scenic spot especially at dusk, when the setting sun silhouettes the high bluffs. The north entrance of the waterway is marked by two islands, as well as a cove to the west, and paddlers can use either channel to round them. Keep in mind, however, that the narrows is busy with motorboat traffic.

Just south of the islands along the west shore of the narrows is the mouth of a deep bay. Past the mouth, the waterway remains a narrow channel for the next 1.3 miles, until it opens up just north of King Williams Campground.

At the beginning of portage to Mukooda Lake

KING WILLIAMS CAMPGROUND: One of two group campgrounds in Voyageurs National Park, the area has a number of tables and fire rings and two covered pit toilets. There is also well water, plenty of space for tents, and a sandy spit ideal for lying around in the sun.

Voyageurs National Park ends at King Williams Campground; beyond it lies Superior National Forest. The large island just south of the campground is Indian Island, with a campsite on its north end and a second in the middle of its west side. It is a 2.5-mile paddle from King Williams Campground to the U.S. Customs Office on Crane Lake.

NAMAKAN LAKE: NAMAKAN NARROWS TO KETTLE FALLS

Distance: 13.5 miles
Portages: 2
Longest portage: 0.2 mile
Paddling time: 6–9 hours

If you are starting from one of the cluster of VNP campsites north of Namakan Narrows, it is possible to paddle the Canadian side of Namakan Lake to Kettle Falls in one day, using Bear River Portage as a shortcut. This would eliminate spending a night on the Canadian side and having to purchase a Crown Land camping permit.

You enter Canada as soon as you cross the Namakan Narrows, which the international boundary divides. Immediately to the east along the Canadian shoreline are a large island and the channel it forms with the mainland. Beyond the island the shoreline is straight and unbroken for the next mile until you reach a peninsula jutting out. Much of the shoreline on the south side of Namakan Lake is steep, rugged, and not conducive to landing a boat or pitching a tent.

The tip of the peninsula is marked by a cabin half-hidden among the trees. Beyond it you can either drop south into the cove the peninsula forms and paddle northeast into the mouth of the Namakan River, or head north to continue following the east side of the lake. Namakan River is usually paddled downstream from Lac La Croix as part of a trip that includes Little Vermilion Narrows, Loon River, and Loon Lake. But an interesting side trip would be to paddle 3 miles upstream to view Lady Rapids, the first stretch of white water from the west end of the river.

If you paddle 0.6 mile due north from the cabin on the south shore you will cross the mouth of Namakan River and then pass through a gap formed by an island to the west and a peninsula from the mainland to the east. Once through the gap you will see a cove to the east with Berger's Trading Post located in the back of it. The trading post, which sells limited groceries and live bait, is run by Betty Lessard, a year-round resident of the lake. The spirited woman is in her eighties and has spent most of her life on Namakan Lake. The outpost is worth stopping at if for no other reason than to listen to her bear stories or to view her collection of Indian spearheads, pieces of pottery, and other artifacts that she has picked up from the lake shore.

North of the cove and Berger's Trading Post is a group of islands, several of which have cabins on them, situated in and near the entrance of a small bay. Cross the bay and you will arrive at the entrance of a long inlet that extends east. Several islands block the entrance, making it difficult to distinguish the body of water. At this point the shoreline of Namakan Lake curves to the west and paddlers will discover a different terrain on the north side. Much of the shoreline on this side of the lake is less steep and rugged than the south shore and features numerous places to beach and camp.

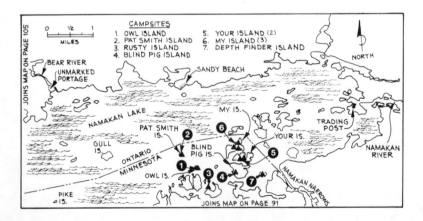

Paddling west, you will spot an island in the distance just offshore. The island lies 2.8 miles due west and marks the halfway point to Bear River. It sits toward the west end of a shallow cove, providing protection from the surf and making it an attractive area for anglers. On the west side of the cove is a sandy strip with a good camping spot among the pines behind it.

Just a few strokes west of the island a bay angles off northeast. From its narrow entrance it is 2.4 miles across two bays to the Bear River Portage. The second is 1.6 miles wide and has eight islands situated in the center of it. Once you are between the islands and the mainland you will spot the white boathouse of Allen Kielczewski, a commercial fisherman who, with his son, fishes the Canadian waters of Namakan Lake.

Just west of their place, next to a rocky point jutting out from the center of the bay, is the mouth of Bear River. Once you make the short portage you are only 3.6 miles away from Kettle Falls. The alternative is to keep paddling west and then head north through Squaw Narrows before curving east through Squirrel Narrows to Kettle Falls, for a total paddle of 11 miles.

BEAR RIVER PORTAGE (Rating—easy; distance—0.1 mile): The portage isn't marked but is easy to spot on the west side of the river. The dry, level path swings around the blocked mouth of Bear River and a small series of rapids to a put-in on the north side.

Bear River

Bear River begins as a narrow and sometimes shallow waterway in its first mile but is navigable by canoes and kayaks. There is much beaver activity in the area and paddlers might be forced to drag their boats across a newly constructed dam. The weedy pools and marsh areas you will pass are tempting spots to toss a line in for a northern pike.

Gradually Bear River opens up to a wide body of water, still flowing in a northerly direction, with marsh areas highlighting both shores. At its widest point the river swings to the northeast and narrows down slightly for the next 0.5 mile until you arrive at its north end. Straight ahead is an island with a huge two-story log cabin on it. Here you have a choice of three channels. You can explore the marshy cove that lies east of the mouth of Bear River or head northeast into the channel that leads to Hale Bay. The route to Kettle Falls is the channel to the northwest.

Red buoys mark the channel toward Kettle Falls. It is a 1.8-mile paddle from the north end of Bear River to the falls, during which you will pass south of four prominent islands. The first one is the largest and has several cabins on its south side. Just east of this island is the Canadian Channel, which leads north into Rainy Lake.

From the south side of the fourth island you can hear the roar of the water rushing out of Kettle Falls dam. At this point canoers and kayakers might want to circle behind the small island instead of trying to paddle straight for the Kettle Falls Portage, which is located in a small cove just north of the dam. The closer you approach the dam the more turbulent the water becomes.

KETTLE FALLS PORTAGE (Rating—easy; distance—0.2 mile): The cove just north of the dam features docks for motorboaters and usually much activity, as it lies just east of the historic Kettle Falls Hotel. A marked gravel road swings to the American waters on the west side of the dam.

Kettle Falls

Kettle Falls today looks much as it did in its heyday in the 1920s, when it was bustling with loggers and miners, and notables such as John D. Rockefeller and Charles Lindbergh passed through. The hotel, with its badly warped floors, old nickelodeon, and long sitting porch is on the National Register of Historical Sites, as is the surrounding area known as the Kettle Falls Historic District.

The 20-room hotel is sound, but over the years all the windows and doors have tilted and dirt washed down from the hill behind it has heaved the floor into its rolling state. A wood stove from the main lobby still provides much of the heat during chilly summer evenings. The hotel closes when the summer tourist season ends in late September.

Nearby there is a short trail to the Kettle Falls dam, where you can watch the waters of the international lakes rush through, dropping 10 feet from Namakan Lake to Rainy Lake. There is also a picnic area, with tables and covered pit toilets, on the western edge of the cove you paddle into from the Canadian side. Occasionally paddlers arriving late in the evening will camp there.

NAMAKAN LAKE: KETTLE FALLS TO ASH RIVER

Distance: 16.4 miles
Portages: 3
Longest portage: 0.6 mile
Paddling time: 2 days

The Kettle Falls Portage will bring you back to American waters, where to the west is a handful of cabins along the north shore and Canada's Kettle Island to the south. After a few strokes you will pass the tip of the peninsula that the cabins lie on and the western end of Kettle Island and enter an open stretch of water. At this point there will be two small islands to the south and then the much larger Squirrel Island. Straight ahead, almost due west of the Kettle Falls dam, is a VNP campsite.

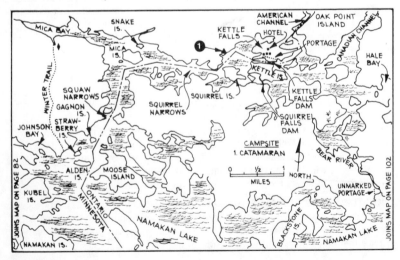

CATAMARAN CAMPSITE: The campsite is located on a small inlet on the Kabetogama Peninsula, where anglers occasionally hook a northern pike along the shore. There is a table, dock, fire ring, open pit toilet, and usually a good breeze blowing through. At the back of the inlet, just through the trees, are a large beaver dam and pond.

The campsite marks the spot where you swing south into the gap between the Kabetogama Peninsula and Squirrel Island and then in a few strokes swing west again into the small opening of Squirrel Narrows. Paddlers might get momentarily confused at this spot because to the southeast is a much wider channel that circles behind Squirrel Island and east toward Canada's Squirrel Falls Dam.

Heading west in the Narrows you will see Mica Island and its orange marker and Snake Island, the smaller of the two, situated to the north. Mica Island picked up its name when two prospectors discovered a vein of the clear crystal rock in 1895, a time when it was used in windows, lamp shades and electrical insulators. The two men put a mica claim on the island and later sank a shaft in attempts to mine it, but the operation was short-lived.

It is 1.5 miles from the entrance of Squirrel Narrows to Mica Island, which sits in the middle of a wide junction. To the west of it is Mica Bay and the interior route to Beast Lake, Brown Lake, and eventually Rainy Lake (see chapter 10 for route description). To the south, after a 1-mile paddle past two large coves on the American shore, you will reach Squaw Narrows. The small channel in Namakan Lake is formed by an oddly shaped peninsula on the Canadian side and an island just off the Kabetogama Peninsula on the American side.

Once through the narrows you will spot a small island to the south and then the larger Gagnon Island 0.25 mile beyond. Gagnon sits outside the entrance to a V-shaped cove from which the lake shore begins to swing more to the west toward Johnson Bay. After passing three islands to the east, the last two Strawberry and Alden, you will see a snowmobile marker on the shoreline just before you paddle into the entrance of the bay. The winter route heads north 2.3 miles to Mica Bay, but crosses too any wetlands and ponds to be tackled in the summer. You can hike the first 0.5 mile, however, to view a large beaver pond and perhaps some of the white-tailed deer that feed along the edge.

The wide entrance to Johnson Bay is just to the south, with five islands in and around it. The bay extends 1 mile to the west, narrowing down in the middle and then opening back up where another island is located deep inside, making it an ideal hideaway from the popular route to Kettle Falls. Continuing south you will leave the bay by paddling between two small islands off its southeast corner and immediately be confronted with a full view of Kubel Island's north shore.

The west side of the large island forms a mile-long channel with the Kabetogama Peninsula, and its east shore features numerous small coves and points (see map on page 82). Hugging the north shore of Namakan Lake you will paddle the channel and sweep past a small island to the south, with the larger Sexton Island just below it. To the southeast you will spot one end of Namakan Island and due west a distinctive peninsula extending south. This section may appear confusing with its many islands and channels to the south, but it is nothing that a quick compass reading and map check can't solve.

When rounding the peninsula you will see the northern end of Williams Island 0.5 mile to the south, and just east of it one end of Stevens Island. Two channels, one on each side of Stevens Island, lead toward the VNP campsites on the south

Eagle's nest

shore of Namakan Island or into the entrances of Hoist or Junction bays. Cemetery Island, described earlier, is west of the peninsula's end.

The channel between Cemetery Island and the Kabetogama Peninsula is wide and features three small islets in a row. The islet farthest to the north has a cabin on it. Following Cemetery Island's shoreline you will pass the west end of Indian Point and head toward Tar Point. Directly west of Indian Point is the portage across Tar Point.

TAR POINT PORTAGE (Rating—easy; distance—0.2 mile): The portage, marked at both ends by a snowmobile sign, takes you up and over the ridge that runs down the middle of Tar Point. It is a winter route and of little use to paddlers in the summer since it's far easier to paddle around the point than to carry your boat over it.

As you round Tar Point to the south you'll see Day Marker 23 Island and Sweetnose Island just to the east of it. The gap between the two allows you to paddle into Blind Indian Narrows, with Moose Bay to the east. Along with the day marker you will also spot the VNP campsite. At one time there was a fish camp on the island, and the workers used to discard their syrup cans on the island next to it—hence its name, Sweetnose.

DAY MARKER 23 ISLAND CAMPSITE: The pleasant campsite, located at the northern tip of the island, has a good view and usually a good breeze running through it to keep it bug free. The site is among a stand of red and white pine and provides a table, fire ring, open pit toilet, and plenty of tent space.

If you continue to follow the shoreline of the Kabetogama Peninsula you will come to the west side of Tar Point and then pass a pair of islands with cabins on them before entering the narrow mouth of Kohler Bay. The 1.2-mile-long bay is a calm and generally quiet body of water. Much of its shoreline supports marsh grass and the whole bay is a haven for northern pike. Just over halfway along the north shore is a small point that could be used as a camping spot.

Toward the back on the south shore is a Kohler Bay Portage. The trail cuts across the narrow neck of the large peninsula that forms the south shore of Kohler Bay and ends at the Kabetogama Narrows, 2 miles east of the VNP Information Station.

KOHLER BAY PORTAGE (Rating—easy; distance—0.3 miles): The level path runs a direct course from the bay to the Kabetogama Narrows and is marked on both ends by snowmobile signs. During the summer it can be wet in the middle, making rubber boots necessary.

If you elect to paddle south from Tar Point, past Day Marker 23 Island, you will enter Blind Indian Narrows and come to the shoreline of the mainland. Paddling to the west you will cross two V-shaped coves and pass two islands with islets next to them. To the north you will see the much larger Ziski Island and then Lone Squaw Island.

After the second island and cove, the shoreline curves south into Old Dutch Bay. It is hard to tell where Namakan Lake ends and Old Dutch Bay begins. There is a VNP campsite on both sides of the bay.

OLD DUTCH BAY CAMPSITE: A secluded campsite is situated deep in the bay on its east side and away from its busy entrance. The site includes a table, fire ring, and open pit toilet, along with a sandy strip on one side for beaching your boat.

NAMAKAN LAKE ENTRANCE CAMPSITE: This one is located on a rock bluff on the west side of the bay near the narrow entrance into Namakan Lake. The site provides a table, fire ring, and open pit toilet, but the waters in front of it can be busy at times.

Due north of the campsite is a roundish island with several cabins on it and a small peninsula extending south from Kabetogama Peninsula. At the tip of the small peninsula is a white sign proclaiming that you are entering Namakan Lake. West of it the waterway opens up for 0.5 mile until you reach a second gap.

The second gap is formed by a large head extending north from the mainland and marked on its east side by two islets. Paddle around it and on the other side is the snowmobile marker for the Sullivan Bay Portage.

SULLIVAN BAY PORTAGE (Rating—difficult; distance—0.6 mile): The portage cuts across the long arm of land that forms the north shore of Sullivan Bay. It begins in a small, sandy cove off of Kabetogama Narrows and ends in marsh area on the bay side. It is a winter trail so snowmobilers and skiers can avoid the weak ice that forms on the narrow channel into Sullivan Bay. Paddlers will find it a difficult and wet trail to hike.

It is almost another mile to the narrow channel leading into Sullivan Bay, called Ash River by many local residents. The Kabetogama Narrows Information Station is 0.5 mile west. The channel is a scenic paddle, with its high cliff walls on both sides, but paddlers have to keep a watchful eye out for motorboaters. Between a handful of resorts on the west end of Sullivan Bay and those on Ash River, the waterway sees more than its share of traffic.

Once in the large bay it is a 3-mile paddle across to the east and down Ash River to the public landing. It is best to hug either the north or south shore if paddling and to stay out of the center lanes, which are used by motorboat traffic.

10   KABETOGAMA PENINSULA

All visitors to Voyageurs National Park begin and end their trip on one of the large lakes. But for many paddlers the destination and reward for all their efforts is the Kabetogama Peninsula, the heart of the park. In this roadless landmass, they find the lonely lake they are seeking, the intimate encounter with nature that they cherish, the adventure they desire.

Trips into the peninsula require more time and energy than those on the large lakes, since more portages and obstacles are encountered. But for visitors searching for wilderness adventure no other section of the park or surrounding area offers as much. The returns for carrying your boat inland are frequent sightings of deer, beaver, black bear, and a variety of other wildlife; the chance to fish in a lake you have all to yourself; and routes that challenge your outdoor skills.

The most popular route is the Chain of Lakes, where paddlers enter the peninsula through Cranberry Creek and travel Locator, War Club, Quill, and Loiten lakes before departing by way of the Kabetogama–Locator Lake Trail. By adding a cross-country portage, backpackers can also paddle the central lakes from Quarter Line to the isolated Shoepack Lake deep in the middle of the peninsula. Or they can travel from Namakan Lake to Rainy Lake by way of Beast, Brown, and Peary lakes, with one trailless portage to tackle. It is even possible to travel the peninsula lengthwise or to cut across it from north to south.

Trips into Kabetogama Peninsula combine the best of what Voyageurs National Park has to offer. You begin your excursion on the large lakes with uninterrupted paddles and island campsites that offer sweeping views of the open scenery around them. You climax it by reaching some isolated corner of the peninsula for a satisfying sense of accomplishment.

No matter what kind of excursion is planned, every visitor should undertake at least one side trip into Kabetogama Peninsula, even if it is only an overnighter to an inland lake. The isolation, ruggedness, and silence of the peninsula does more than soothe minds; it allows us to contemplate where we are, where this land has been, and where we are going with our world.

CHAIN OF LAKES: CRANBERRY BAY TO SHOEPACK LAKE

Distance: 14.6 miles
Portages: 4
Longest portage: 2 miles
Paddling time: 2–3 days

Paddlers entering and departing the Chain of Lakes by either trail to Locator Lake should consider routing their trip into the peninsula by way of Cranberry Bay and the portage to Cranberry Creek to avoid backtracking. This portage is shorter and has less climbing than the Locator Lake Trail, which is easier to undertake near the end of your trip after you've consumed some of your supplies.

For those beginning at Island View it is best to stop at the island the NPS refers to as Diamond Island or at Cranberry Creek Campsite the first day and undertake the portage into Locator Lake early the next day (see chapter 11 for route description from Island View to Diamond Island). The paddle from Island

View to the Locator Lake Campsite, a 12-mile trip, is a long day that finishes with a grueling portage.

There are no shortcuts from the west side of Diamond Island into Cranberry Bay through the narrow gaps shown on topographical maps. Those channels southwest of the island are filled with marsh grass and impassable by canoe or kayak. From Diamond Island Campsite paddle east to the tip of the island's lower arm and then pass a small island where the remains of an old vehicle, stranded for the last 30 years, can be seen.

Round the island and head south, passing a small cove with the rusted-out body of a 1920s truck on one side. This cove is formed by the small island and a larger one to the south, and in the back you will notice the rocky gap between the two. Follow the east side of this larger island and you will enter a channel that leads into Cranberry Bay. The east side of the waterway is formed by Arden Island.

You'll go from the narrow channel into the wide expanse of Cranberry Bay, where a strong wind has enough open water to create large waves. Almost straight across, there is a huge, round, white granite erratic along the south shore of the bay. The 200-ton rock is evidence of the glaciers that shaped much of the park and left this stone in its conspicuous setting.

Paddle west from Arden Island. Within a mile the bay narrows to a gap and then curves sharply to the south. Just before reaching it, you will see a group of small islands along the north shore that have been filled in by marsh grass. This is what remains of the channels that at one time led to the west side of Diamond Island. Once through the gap, the bay heads south and becomes much shallower with extensive marsh areas along both shores. Keep a sharp eye out for wildlife—the bay is a haven for waterfowl and other bird life.

Many paddlers follow the east shore of the bay closely and then find themselves either getting stuck in shallow water or mistaking a V-shaped cove for the entrance of Cranberry Creek. The best route is to paddle down the middle and watch the western shoreline for where it takes a sharp curve west. At this point you will have a good view of the bay's backside and should spot the mouth of the creek to the south, as one side is marked by a high bluff.

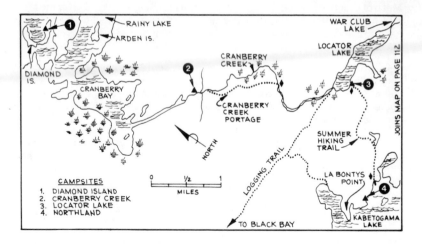

Beaver dam near Cranberry Creek

The stream is a delightful sight and a welcome change of scenery for those who have just struggled through the marsh grass and shallow water of the bay. Much of Cranberry Creek's shoreline is composed of high banks, and for the first mile from its entrance it flows in a straight, southeasterly direction for an easy paddle. Eventually you paddle past a small cove on the east shore, round two bends in the creek, and then arrive at a VNP campsite.

CRANBERRY CREEK CAMPSITE: Situated on a high bluff along the east shore, the campsite has a postcard view of the creek to the northwest, allowing you to view the waterway you just paddled almost to its entrance on the bay. There is a table, fire ring, and covered pit toilet, and you will have few bugs to contend with during June and July.

———————————

Cranberry Creek continues from the campsite in a southeast direction and quickly comes to a junction with two streams facing each other. They might be difficult to spot during a dry spell. After that you will come to an old beaver dam. The section in the middle has collapsed, but paddlers have little choice but to get out and drag their boats through.

You'll pass two more bends in the creek and then round a flat grassy point on the west shore, marked at the end by a large pine tree. In front of you will be a shallow set of rapids and to the west the unmarked beginning of the portage to the lower half of Cranberry Creek.

It is possible to skip much of the portage and paddle a canoe or kayak through Cranberry Creek. This should be attempted by those with a high sense of adventure in an empty boat on a reasonably calm day. No one should attempt this with the idea of saving time or energy—you will not.

You will get wet up to your knees and will be overwhelmed by bugs during July. But paddling this stretch will give you a chance to see some amazing beaver dams and lodges and perhaps other wildlife, including a rare moose, along the waterway.

Pull your boat out at the Cranberry Creek Portage Trail to bypass the rapids. A natural trail leads from the portage trail back to the creek just beyond the small rapids. From here you will most likely have to work your way around fallen trees until you reach the first of four dams you will encounter before the stream divides into two channels. Even though the fork to the northeast appears to be the main channel, stay to the southeast, where you will encounter a fifth dam.

At this point begin to look for a spot to come ashore and search for the trail, which lies just southwest of the stream. The farther you paddle up Cranberry Creek the steeper the gorge becomes, making the climb to the portage trail a difficult trek. Eventually an entanglement of fallen trees and a small waterfall deep in the gorge prevent you from paddling to the south end of the portage without spending an enormous amount of energy to get around them.

CRANBERRY CREEK PORTAGE (Rating—moderate; distance—1.3 miles): The trail hugs the creek for the first 100 yards and then swings away to a partially planked wet area almost 0.5 mile from the beginning. You'll pass near Cranberry Creek again, where a side trail can be followed to view a large beaver lodge. Immediately after that the portage trail crosses an old grass-covered beaver dam.

At this point the trail begins to climb, gently at first and then more rapidly for the next 0.3 mile. You follow the high area until it breaks out to a scenic view of Cranberry Creek, a slow-moving stream now winding its way through the tall grasses of a marsh. From here it is a rapid walk down to the creek where the south end of the portage is marked.

From the south end of the portage Cranberry Creek is a deep stream that wanders 1.2 miles through a marsh grass valley. This stretch is a beautiful sight in late afternoon on a clear day, with the dark brown creek meandering slowly through the field of tall grass turned shades of gold and yellow by the lowering sun. Having hauled their boats over the portage trail, most paddlers find this section of the creek into Locator Lake a very enjoyable one. There are many tight bends and curves to work around, but no beaver obstruction that will force you to step out of your boat.

LOCATOR LAKE AND CAMPSITE: Eventually Cranberry Creek curves around a tree-lined bluff on the north side and you paddle into Locator Lake, where you can see its entire 1.3-mile length. On the south side of the creek just before it flows into the lake is the winter trail that heads 2.5 miles to an arm of Black Bay. A spur south of it leads to a bay on Kabetogama Lake. The trails are used primarily during the winter by skiers and snowmobilers, but hikers can also explore them with the help of 14-inch rubber boots.

Locator, the largest of the Chain of Lakes, is 52 feet deep and 0.5 mile wide at a narrow inlet off the south shore. Anglers can try their luck for northern pike in Locator, especially around the weedy shoreline of the arm. Most of the lake's shoreline is composed of high banks or even bluffs, making it difficult to camp anywhere but the VNP campsite on the south shore. One bluff along the north shore, almost directly across from the lake's southern arm, is the site of a scenic little waterfall.

When entering the lake from Cranberry Creek, cut across it in a southeast direction and look for the wooden staircase that marks the Locator Lake Campsite, 0.25 mile away. The site is situated high above the water and serves as one end of the Locator Lake Trail, which heads south 1.6 miles to Kabetogama Lake (see chapter 13 for description). The site provides a table, fire ring, and covered pit toilet, but has limited space for tents. A pleasant evening can be spent watching the sun set over the northwest corner of the lake from the staircase.

WAR CLUB LAKE AND CAMPSITE: The paddle east toward War Club is an easy one, especially if a northwest wind springs up. The shoreline of Locator gradually narrows down to the short stream that connects the two inland lakes. The stream is narrow, but is free of any beaver construction as it passes through a gorge to the west end of War Club. War Club is almost as long as Locator but not nearly as wide and only 40 feet deep. High bluffs and banks make up most of the shoreline, limiting camping to the VNP campsite along the north shore. Two shallow coves lie near the west end on the north shore; a third, much smaller one a little farther east, is the site of the VNP campsite.

The War Club Lake Campsite is situated above the water and offers good views of both ends of the lake, but not much tent space. Beaver activity from the cove east may provide entertainment during dinner, since you can sit at the table and watch them swim across the lake. The campsite includes a fire ring, and covered pit toilet.

QUILL LAKE PORTAGE (Rating—easy; distance—150 yards): The small stream that flows from Quill can be found in the middle of a marsh area at the east end of War Club. Almost as soon as you enter it there is one beaver dam, then two more a little farther up. Caution should be used stepping over the dams or you'll end up in water to your waist.

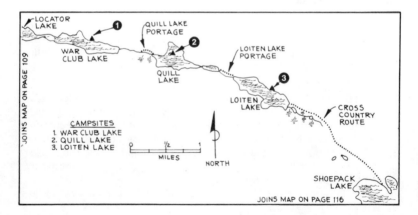

Kayaker pulling his boat over a beaver dam on his way to Quill Lake

After the third dam the stream narrows down and you will hear the rustle of a small waterfall. Look to the north for the portage trail that follows a well-worn path along the side of the stream, climbing the entire way to Quill Lake's higher elevation. Entering Quill Lake from the trail can also be tricky as there is more beaver obstruction where the outlet stream begins.

QUILL LAKE AND CAMPSITE: Quill is a pretty little lake with a steep, forested shoreline and an island sitting practically in the middle of it. The 92-acre lake is 0.8 mile long and almost 0.5 mile at its widest point, with clear water that reaches a maximum depth of 46 feet. Anglers who portage a boat in will be rewarded with northern pike, rock bass, yellow perch, and largemouth bass. Those who arrive early in the summer should concentrate their fishing around the small pond just east of the lake and the cove in the southwest corner where a beaver lodge is located.

At the eastern end a high rock bluff along the north shore rises steeply for over 140 feet. A quick scramble up the bluff will give you a clear view of the entire lake. Just east of the bluff is the small strip of land that divides Quill Lake from the pond into which the stream from Loiten Lake flows. It is possible in an empty boat to skim over a narrow gap in the strip, but the paddlers of loaded canoes might have to step out and drag their boat through.

The campsite is on the southeast corner of the island and is one of VNP's gems, worthy of an extra day. It provides a fire ring, table, and covered pit toilet, and catches any breeze on the lake surface, reducing the number of bugs. From the island you can view the entire lake and at dusk spot any wildlife such as beaver, deer, or loons, swimming in the water or feeding along the shoreline.

LOITEN LAKE PORTAGE (Rating—moderate; distance—0.25 mile): By paddling to the east end of Quill Lake and then through the small pond beyond it, you will come to the stream that empties from Loiten Lake. On the north side of the stream is the unmarked but easy to locate portage trail to the next lake. It is often described as the hardest 0.25-mile trail in the park. The path is level but is covered with large boulders and with trees brought down by either beavers or high winds. When carrying a boat across, you have to be extremely careful to avoid possible injury from slipping on a wet boulder or loose log.

The trail is in poor condition, often wet and plagued by bugs, but it is only 0.25 mile long. You have to walk only 100 yards to begin seeing your reward—Loiten Lake.

LOITEN LAKE AND CAMPSITE: This is the fourth lake in the chain and the highest one, with an elevation of 1188 feet. The 90-acre lake is almost 1 mile long and 0.3 mile at its widest point. Its largest cove lies near the southeast corner. Most of the shoreline is composed of high bluffs, which limit camping to the VNP campsite on the north shore. The campsite has been moved from its earlier location on the east shore.

There are two beaver ponds at the east end of the lake. The first is located in the northeast corner, where the old dam is overgrown by grass and brush. You can hop out of your boat onto the dam to see the pond, lodge, and surrounding grassy area behind it. There are usually moose tracks and droppings around the pond in the grassy area.

The other beaver pond is at the east end of the lake. You have to hike 100 yards across a forested strip of land before you come to what appears to be a large pond. This is the beginning of 0.5 mile of marsh and ponds that makes an excellent place to spot wildlife. The other way to view this stretch is to climb up the bluff that runs along it to the north. There are several places on the bluff from which you can see the entire marsh area.

The Loiten Lake Campsite is now located on the north shore two-thirds of the way to the east end, almost directly across from the lake's largest cove on the south shore (old park maps show its previous location). The site provides a table, fire ring, covered pit toilet, and a view of most of the lake.

LOITEN LAKE TO SHOEPACK LAKE PORTAGE (Rating—difficult; distance—2 miles): At this point the vast majority of paddlers turn around, backtrack to Locator Lake, and exit the peninsula by the Locator Lake Trail or by way of Cranberry Creek. But for those with past experience in cross-country travel who are looking for an outdoor challenge, it is possible to travel from Loiten Lake to Shoepack. Portaging a boat across this route is difficult but not impossible if two people work together and plan to spend an entire day moving from one lake to the other.

Nobody should try this cross-country route on the spur of the moment. The crossing requires a good knowledge of map and compass and a tag bag (see chapter 6) of 400 to 500 orange flags to mark a course so you can return to portage the boat. What follows is a very brief, general description of the route—*it is not intended as a guide to Shoepack Lake.* Those who attempt this adventure will find their own routes—that is the challenge of cross-country travel.

If it is winter, the easiest route to Shoepack is the L-shaped string of marshes, ponds, and streams beginning in the southeast corner of Loiten that link the two lakes together. But the easiest and driest route during the summer begins at the east end of the lake, where a large boulder sits on the shoreline.

From the boulder it is a steady climb to the top of the ridge that runs southeast toward Shoepack. Take a compass reading of 126 degrees and use it to follow

An early morning breakfast of bass from Quill Lake

the ridge. The next 0.5 mile is not difficult as you follow the crest of the ridge, which occasionally opens up to a view of the two beaver ponds and marsh area to the south. Several times you drop into heavy forested sections or even wet areas before returning to bare rock ridge for another view of the marsh area.

Eventually you will spot the second beaver pond and shortly after that the marsh will turn into a small stream and then disappear into the woods. You will continue in the same direction and work your way to the head of the valley—and possibly through a muskeg swamp area if you swing too far south—before beginning a slight descent.

If you keep to the high ground of the ridge you will pass another pair of ponds to the south. Stay north of both the ponds and the marsh area around them. Once past them change your course to almost a due south direction, and in another 0.3 mile you should break out on the shore of Shoepack—where you can celebrate your accomplishment.

Shoepack is a large lake and hard to miss. If you maintain your course you should break out somewhere near its northwest corner, where the long, narrow peninsula extends 0.25 mile into the lake. Keep in mind during the trip that there are no trails in this section between the two lakes. Anything that resembles one is a path formed by browsing deer or moose.

CENTRAL LAKES: LOST BAY TO SHOEPACK LAKE

Distance: 5.3 miles
Portages: 4
Longest portage: 1.4 miles
Paddling time: 1–2 days

This is the easiest and quickest route to Shoepack Lake. Paddlers could complete the entire trip in one day, but it would be a long day as the 1.4-mile portage from Jorgens to Little Shoepack Lake involves some cross-country travel and taking an old logging road through wet areas. Most backpackers are coming here from another section of the park and stop at Jorgens Lake before they complete the journey into Shoepack Lake the next day.

Vegetable matter from the swampy areas that drain into it have turned Shoepack into one of the brownest lakes in the park—which makes for fine reflections of the shoreline but not for good drinking water. Plan to boil the water for a full three minutes or, as many backpackers do, carry some water inland from Lost Bay.

QUARTER LINE LAKE PORTAGE (Rating—moderate; distance—0.5 mile): The trail is picked up either from Eks Bay Campsite or at the end of the inlet to the west of it. From the campsite the first 200 yards follow the high bank of the western inlet before dipping at its end, which is blocked by a large beaver dam. The dam and pond are crossed by planking, at which point the trail reenters the forest and quickly arrives at a marked intersection. The trail to the east departs for Ek Lake Campsite, 1.5 miles away, and eventually the Cruiser Lake Trail.

Straight ahead is the trail to Quarter Line. It climbs over three ridges, of which the second is by far the steepest. After climbing the third ridge you arrive at another posted junction. Due north 0.6 mile is Jorgens Lake. To the east is the spur to Quarter Line Lake which drops off the ridge for the next 0.2 mile and curves around to the western end of the lake.

QUARTER LINE LAKE AND CAMPSITE: Quarter Line is a small lake, 0.3 mile in length with murky, brown water that reaches a maximum depth of only 22 feet. Many backpackers elect to boil the water of Quarter Line, Jorgens, and Little Shoepack rather than trust their filter system. At the east end, where the lake widens, it's possible to sit in a boat at dusk and watch beavers swim back and forth, or to fish for the northern pike that like to hang out in the small cove in the

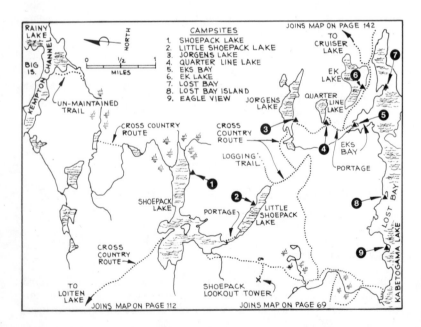

southeast corner. The west end narrows down to a beaver dam where pike might also lurk.

The spur to Quarter Line Lake ends right at the VNP campsite, situated near the beaver dam at the west end. The site provides a table, fire ring, and open pit toilet, but not a whole lot of space to pitch a tent. The flattest area lies west of the campsite toward the dam.

JORGENS LAKE PORTAGE (Rating—moderate; distance—0.6 mile): The trail is 0.6 mile from the junction with the spur to Quarter Line Lake or 0.8 mile if you are starting from the small lake. From the junction, head north along the trail that runs level for a brief spell before dipping to cross a planked low area. The trail then begins a steep ascent and levels out as it crosses a bare rock crest. From here it will drop and ascend two more ridges with a planked wet area between them. After the third ascent the path drops to the campsite near the west end of the lake.

JORGENS LAKE AND CAMPSITE: Jorgens is almost 1 mile in length, covers 64 acres, and has a maximum depth of 21 feet. Northern pike are present throughout the lake, and there is usually some beaver activity near dusk at both ends. Jorgens narrows down at its east end where bluffs border it. At the west end is a pair of coves surrounded by an extensive marsh area.

The VNP campsite is situated on the south shore near the west end. The site provides a table, fire ring, open pit toilet, and tent pads, since there is little level space elsewhere to pitch a tent.

JORGENS LAKE TO LITTLE SHOEPACK LAKE PORTAGE (Rating—difficult; distance—1.4 miles): This route is not nearly as difficult as the 2-mile cross-country portage from Loiten Lake to Shoepack. It does involve negotiating a 0.5-mile stretch across a heavily wooded ridge and searching out an old logging trail, but if backpackers take their time and start early in the day they should encounter few problems reaching Little Shoepack Lake.

Begin by paddling the long narrow inlet at the west end of Jorgens Lake. You will have to wind through the floating marsh brush and then beach your boat on the north side when you reach the dam. From here walk the fine line between the young aspen trees and the older pines farther up the shore for the next 100 yards. You will break out at a flat grassy area that on most maps is depicted as a pond.

The grassy area still resembles the pond on the map and you should cross it along what used to be the north shore. To the south there is a beaver lodge and a small pond behind it; between you and the lodge is a large, prominent rock. Stay north of the rock and make your way to what used to be a cove on the west side of the grassy area. From the center of this old cove you will cut across the ridge that lies between you and the logging road into Little Shoepack Lake.

Follow a due west course across the ridge. The aspen trees will be thick in the beginning but gradually thin out as you ascend to the top of the ridge. Depending on where you started and your line of travel, you might be able to look out and see the other side of the ravine as well as the steep west side of the ridge. Head down the ridge into an open grassy area and from here begin searching for the old logging trail in a due west direction.

The old trail is distinguishable but is overgrown in some spots by young aspen trees. It's important to remember that the tote road heads to Little Shoepack in a northwest direction after forming a sharp V-shaped curve in the ravine. The other half of the V departs due west and without a compass reading, it would be easy to mistake one for the other.

The tote road climbs steadily and the sides of the ravine close in on it. After 0.3 mile its pitch increases until it levels out where backpackers will find some sections of standing water and mud, a sign that you are nearing the lake. Eventually the trees thin out and you come to a fork, with one spur curving north and the other departing straight ahead for the east end of Little Shoepack Lake.

Those traveling from Little Shoepack to Jorgens Lake will have an easier time as they can quickly pick up the logging trail by beginning at the rock bluff in the southeast corner of the lake. From the bluff cut across the marsh area to south, staying 25 yards within the shoreline at the end of the lake to cross the tote road. Once on the old logging trail, hike 0.6 mile southeast and then begin to cut across the ridge to reach the grassy marsh area just west of Jorgens Lake.

LITTLE SHOEPACK LAKE AND CAMPSITE: Little Shoepack is a long, narrow lake, a mile long and 29 feet at its maximum depth. There are three islets at its northwest end where fishermen can try their luck among the weed beds for northern pike. There are also muskellunge for those anglers with enough patience and time.

The Little Shoepack Lake Campsite is located toward the middle of its northeast shoreline near a small marshy cove. The site provides a table and a stand-up grill, but tent space is limited. Those planning to reach the lake between mid-July and August should bring pancake mix—the rocky shoreline the campsite is situated on is covered with blueberry bushes.

LITTLE SHOEPACK LAKE TO SHOEPACK LAKE PORTAGE (Rating—easy; distance—0.25 mile): Paddle into the inlet at the northwest end of Little Shoepack Lake, right to the beaver dam, and pull onto the rocky shore on the north side (to the right). There is a short path that connects the two lakes, but it begins on the other side of the dam, so there is little alternative but to haul your boat 20 yards through the thick growth of aspen on the side of the hill to clear the dam. The path hugs the stream right to the southern tip of Shoepack Lake.

SHOEPACK LAKE AND CAMPSITE: Shoepack is the largest lake on the Kabetogama Peninsula, measuring 1 mile wide and 1.75 miles long. It has three arms and a large island almost in the center of where they come together. The lake has a maximum depth of 24 feet, and most of its 6-mile shoreline is surrounded by marsh areas and swamps. Shoepack is known for its muskellunge population, which the Minnesota Department of Natural Resources at one time used as brood stock to supply eggs for its artificial propagation program.

The portage from Little Shoepack emerges at the end of the southern arm. Paddle north a few strokes and to the west you will spot an old, boarded-up cabin. Behind it are some wide grassy areas that could be used as a camping spot. The Kabetogama–Shoepack Lake Trail also terminates behind the cabin and from this end it is an easy and dry 1.2-mile walk to the Shoepack Lookout for the best view of the park (see chapter 13 for trail description).

Continue to paddle north and you will arrive at the island in the center of the lake, the largest of three in Shoepack. It offers good camping possibilities and is far more scenic and bug-free than the VNP campsite located on the eastern arm of the lake. An arm extending 0.5 mile to the west is formed on one side by a long, narrow peninsula. This is the area where paddlers making the cross-country portage route from Loiten Lake will arrive.

Dead trees in Shoepack Lake

Northeast from the island is the gap leading into the eastern arm. An islet sits in the middle of the gap, making it appear even narrower than it is. Paddle 0.5 mile into the arm toward the third and final island. Almost directly across from it on the south shore is the Shoepack Lake Campsite. The site provides a covered pit toilet, stand-up grill, and a table. It lies just beyond a marsh area and can host more than its share of bugs during the summer. Tent space is limited.

Along the north shore of this eastern arm, northeast of the VNP campsite, is the stream that flows into Rainy Lake. From Shoepack the stream begins as a navigable waterway where you can paddle 0.6 mile north. It is part of a cross-country route that paddlers can use to reach Shoepack from Rainy Lake.

SHOEPACK LAKE FROM THE NORTH

RAINY LAKE TO SHOEPACK LAKE PORTAGE (Rating—difficult; distance—2.6 miles): This route connects Rainy Lake to Shoepack Lake, 2.6 miles to the south, but it is a difficult day's journey involving numerous encounters with beaver dams, long stretches of swamp areas, and a cross-country walk across a ridge. Experienced paddlers who want to attempt this trip should plan on an entire day to move their equipment and boat from Rainy Lake into Shoepack.

The starting point is a small cove located directly across from the southeast corner of Big Island at the east end of Kempton Channel. Paddle to the back of the cove, where you will find a narrow slip extending farther south. In the back of the slip is a waterfall formed by the stream emptying from Shoepack.

An old trail swings near the waterfall and then curves south toward the stream. You can pick it up by starting on the west side of the slip and cutting 25 to 40 feet inland. You might have to search hard to find it. The trail curves away from the slip and cove and in 0.25 mile upstream swings past the bear slide, a slab of granite rock the stream rushes across.

Put in after the bear slide and work your way up the stream as it curves from a south to a westerly direction, continuing around any obstructions. Almost a mile from the bear slide you should reach a small pond. From here the stream heads west in a large U-shaped curve, then doubles back to Shoepack Lake directly south of you. At one time there was an old trail from the pond directly south to the point where the stream curves back.

It is difficult, if not impossible, to locate the trail, and most paddlers just make their way across the ridge due south 0.5 mile to pick up the stream again just before it enters another pond. From here you should be able to make your way to Shoepack through a wider, more navigable waterway with only a few beaver dams to overcome. You end up on the north shore of the lake's eastern arm, almost directly across from the VNP campsite on the south shore.

EASTERN INLAND LAKES: MICA BAY TO RAINY LAKE

Distance: 11.3 miles (including all portages)
Portages: 9
Longest portage: 1.7 miles
Paddling time: 2–3 days

This route between Namakan Lake and Rainy Lake is a pleasant alternative to the more traditional method of crossing over at the often bustling Kettle Falls. It requires moving your boat over numerous portages, including a cross-country route from Beast to Brown Lake, but rewards you with sections of Voyageurs National Park that neither motorboaters nor hikers can reach.

With the 1.2-mile cross-country route from Beast to the Cruiser Lake Trail, it would be extremely difficult to complete this entire trip in one day. It takes most paddlers at least two, and even more days should be scheduled if you plan to spend some time on the various lakes.

West of Mica and Snake Islands is the entrance to Mica Bay, a narrow, 2-mile long body of water that flows from west to east. Following the steep shoreline on the south side you will reach a narrow slip after a 1.3-mile paddle from the bay's mouth. In the back of it is a snowmobile sign. During the summer, hikers with rubber boots can follow the trail for almost a mile, passing some impressive beaver ponds and dams, before extensive marsh area and wetlands force them to turn back.

Another 0.25 mile along the south shore is a stream trickling out into the bay. Look closely for a pair of trails, one on each side of the stream, departing south into the dense forest. This is the portage to Weir Lake.

WEIR LAKE PORTAGE (Rating—moderate; distance—0.6 mile): The trail on the east side of the stream begins as the clearer of the two paths, and after 100 yards it crosses the stream to join the trail on the west side. From here the trail follows the stream as it ascends steadily. Once the path levels out it is possible to cut through the thin line of trees to see an enormous beaver dam blocking the pond north of Weir Lake.

After swinging briefly to the west and then back southwest the trail dead-ends at the beaver pond, since the huge dam has flooded out the remainder to Weir Lake. From this point you have to cut up into the ridge to the west before dropping down at the north cove on Weir Lake.

WEIR LAKE: The small lake, 0.6 mile long, has murky brown water with a maximum depth of only 8 feet. There is no VNP campsite on the lake, but there are camping possibilities next to an old log cabin—or rather half a cabin—on the north cove near where the portage trail ends. From this spot you can see the upper half of the lake. Although anglers would be hard pressed to catch something beyond an occasional pike in Weir Lake, the isolated spot is conducive to sighting wildlife along the shore.

BEAST LAKE PORTAGE (Rating—easy; distance—0.5 mile): Once you have paddled past the trail to Weir Lake, the end of Mica Bay lies less than 0.5 mile to the west. The north shore along this stretch is composed of high bluffs where a line of pine trees crowding the edge looks as if it is on the verge of tumbling into the bay. An old wooden canoe, bottomless and half-filled with water, is situated near the east end of the portage trail to Beast Lake.

The end of the trail in Mica Bay is marked and departs west along a level, well-planked path, surprisingly dry, considering the swampy area it passes through. After crossing the wetlands, the trail rises slightly to the higher level of the lake, levels out, and emerges at the east end of Beast Lake.

BEAST LAKE AND CAMPSITE: Beast is a scenic lake with cold, clear water and a pair of rounded islands situated at its west end. It is long and narrow, measuring a little over 1 mile from east to west and only 0.25 mile at its widest point. It has a maximum depth of 66 feet, and its clear water prompted DNR officials to stock it with trout at one time. It was last stocked in 1980, but the signs that proclaim "no fishing except during trout season" still stand near the portage. There are no walleye or northern pike in the lake and only a few stray

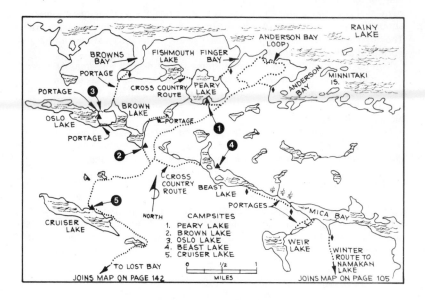

JOINS MAP ON PAGE 142

JOINS MAP ON PAGE 105

rainbow trout left, since the average lifespan of the fish is only eight years. Now that the park area is to be left as much as possible in its natural state, the trout will no longer be stocked.

From the east end it is a 0.5-mile paddle to the tip of the first island. The second island is 0.25 mile west and still shows the charred remains of a fire that swept across most of it. The lake curves north after the second island, directly east of which is the Beast Lake Campsite. The site features a table, stand-up grill, and open pit toilet. Tent space is limited. As with most inland lakes, bugs can be a problem.

BEAST LAKE TO BROWN LAKE PORTAGE (Rating—difficult; distance— 1.7 miles): This portage is rated difficult only because part of it is a cross-country route, covering an area where no trail exists, and because it requires a steep climb in the beginning and a steep descent to Brown Lake at the end. But most of the route is along a ridge top, where the brush is light. The Cruiser Lake Trail crosses its western end. As long as you maintain a westerly heading you will reach the hiking trail.

Those who eye the stream that empties into the west end of Beast Lake as an easy shortcut will think again when they arrive at it and find its mouth blocked by heavy marsh grasses and brush. The route over the ridge is far easier. Take a light load your first trip and mark a route with flags. Return for your boat and remove your flags the last time through.

Begin at the island farther to the west and paddle due south of it to the shoreline. Here you will be faced with a steep climb of 0.2 mile to the top of the ridge through a thick growth of aspen trees and brush. At the top, however, the terrain becomes a pleasant mix of bare rock crest and thin stands of aspen and birch, where the underbrush is not heavy. Deer are often feeding in the area, so it pays to maintain a quiet stride.

Keep a westerly direction and try to stay along the ridge's north side. If you wander too far north you will descend to the stream and two beaver ponds that parallel it; too far to the south you will descend into another marsh area. It should be about a 1-mile hike from the top of the ridge to the Cruiser Lake Trail. The ridge ascends high enough so that at several points you can look back to the northeast and see Rainy Lake.

Don't assume you're lost when you come to some small wet areas on top of the ridge. Eventually you will pass the stream and beaver ponds to the north, though they are rarely seen through the trees. Cruiser Lake Trail crosses the ridge at its western end, where it is often no more than a series of rock cairns along a slab of solid granite.

Most portagers end up north of the junction to Brown Lake and head south on the Cruiser Lake Trail to reach the marked spur. The side trail is a steep 0.5-mile descent to the VNP campsite at the southeastern end of the lake.

BROWN LAKE AND CAMPSITE: The peanut-shaped lake is 0.75 mile long and 0.25 mile at its widest point, with a maximum depth of 27 feet. The VNP campsite is located near its southeastern end, and the portage trail to Browns Bay on Rainy Lake begins at the other end. There are two coves along its west side that extend toward Oslo Lake and a stream that departs from its east side and flows north to Peary Lake. Anglers who portage a boat in will find the lake a good place for northern pike.

The VNP campsite is situated right at the end of the spur from the Cruiser Lake

Peary Lake Campsite

Trail. The site is not marked from the water, but as you near the south end you will be able to spot the table through the trees. There is not much level tent space, but from the table and fire ring you can see the lower half of the lake.

OSLO LAKE—SOUTH PORTAGE (Rating—moderate; distance—0.3 mile): There are two ways to enter Oslo Lake from Brown Lake. If your main goal in life is to avoid portages at all costs you can follow a route through the largest cove to the south. The stream that winds through the marsh area between the two lakes is shallow and narrow. During normal or high water levels however, canoes and kayaks can squeeze through it with just a little extra push here and there. You can almost reach Oslo except for the final 10 yards, where a logjam requires all paddlers to pull their boat through the marsh grass around it and into the lake.

You can also hike this strip by following the north side of the marsh, which is surprisingly dry and matted down. The route is 0.3 mile long, with a very distinct animal trail along most of it.

OSLO LAKE AND CAMPSITE: The long, narrow lake measures 1.2 miles in length and 0.25 mile wide at its east end, and has a maximum depth of 34 feet. There is a large wooded island near its western end. The fact that it is virtually cut off from powerboaters and hikers makes for solitude worth all the effort spent reaching it. Anglers can fish its highly irregular shoreline for northern pike.

The VNP campsite is located at the east end on a point between the two streams that flow into Brown Lake. The site overlooks the eastern half of the lake and provides a table, fire ring, and a tent pad. Level space is scarce.

OSLO LAKE—NORTH PORTAGE (Rating—easy; distance—0.1 mile): This is the easiest way to enter or depart Oslo Lake. The path itself is a hop, skip, and a jump across a neck of land that separates the two lakes. The challenging part comes once you are in Brown Lake. When trying to reach either the portage trail or the rest of Brown Lake, you have to paddle through a marsh area that has a maze of narrow channels running through it. Many come to a dead end, forcing you to back-paddle since there is not enough room to turn around. No matter which direction you are coming from, keep in mind that the best channel through flows along the north side of the marsh.

BROWN LAKE TO BROWNS BAY PORTAGE (Rating—moderate; distance —0.5 mile): The actual trail is easy and dry. What makes this portage difficult is the marsh area that lies between the trail and the open water of Brown Lake. If making your way to Rainy Lake you will paddle as far as you can into the marsh, then have little choice but to hop out and drag your boat across the grass for the next 30 to 40 yards. If you are portaging in from Rainy Lake you begin with the wet walk before a deep channel appears. The alternative to getting wet is to hike along the ridge on the west side, fighting the thick brush instead. It's debatable which is easier.

The trail itself begins with a gradual descent and then levels out to cross a wet area. From here it makes a rapid descent to the lower level of Browns Bay.

BROWN LAKE TO PEARY LAKE PORTAGE (Rating—moderate; distance— 0.4 mile): From the Brown Lake Campsite paddle north into the stream that flows from the northeast corner of the lake. Canoers and kayakers can squeeze past the log at its mouth and then wedge their way through the marshy channel for the next 0.25 mile until they come to a small pond created by a beaver dam. Look to the north side of the dam for the unmarked beginning of the trail.

The rough trail was cut by someone other than VNP rangers and is not a well-worn path, making it confusing to follow in some places. It departs from the beaver dam, climbs over a huge boulder, and then descends sharply to pass near the stream again. From here it curves north through the forest to emerge at a large beaver pond.

At this point the portage is over, but what remains is a 0.5-mile paddle through the beaver pond and adjoining marsh area into Peary Lake. Although you don't have to portage your boat, you will have to hop out and pull it over some obstructions. The first is the large beaver dam that forms the north end of the pond. The best spot to pull your boat over is dead center, where you will enter a narrow channel on the other side.

The channel is narrow but still wide enough to paddle through. It curves and winds its way through the tall marsh grasses until it comes to a second beaver dam. Beyond this dam you paddle a short way and come to the third and final beaver dam. From this one you can view the wide expanse of Peary Lake, and once over it, have a short paddle through the remaining marsh grass to the lake's edge.

PEARY LAKE AND CAMPSITE: The round lake is 0.5 mile in diameter and only 15 feet at its deepest point. But the terrain around it is interesting; a high bluff of bare rock can be scrambled up in its southwest corner for an excellent

Sunset on Brown Lake

view of the area. There is also a high rock bluff on its northeast corner, which the Cruiser Lake Trail traverses. Just offshore from this bluff is an islet of solid rock where you can fry on a hot August day. There is another small island near the lake's northwest corner.

The VNP campsite is on a point in the southeast corner, a 0.25-mile paddle northeast from where you enter the lake from Brown Lake. The site is cramped, with a table and fire ring but almost no space for a tent. Getting out of your boat along the shore can also be tricky as there is no smooth place to land.

FISHMOUTH LAKE AND PORTAGE (Rating—moderate; distance—0.3 mile): Due west from the larger island in Peary Lake is the shortest route to Fishmouth Lake, a small isolated body of water just east of Browns Bay. The 0.3-mile route is basically a climb up and over the ridge that separates the two lakes.

Fishmouth has the distinction of having some of the darkest water within the park, worse than Shoepack. The water in this lake is not brown but black. Once again the reflections can be stunning at times, but paddlers planning to spend a night on its shore should haul in their water from another source. The best camping spot by the lake is on the round point that sticks out to the middle of the lake from the west side.

PEARY LAKE–FINGER BAY PORTAGE (Rating—easy; distance—0.25 mile): A point with a high rock bluff on it extends from Peary Lake's north shore; its east side forms a narrow cove. Paddle into the cove and look to its east shore, across from the bluff, for an unmarked trail. The path descends along with the stream and passes a small waterfall. From here it levels out and comes to the southern end of Finger Bay. The view from this point is impressive, with a slice of Rainy Lake framed by the bay's high, narrow walls.

11 RAINY LAKE

Despite its sometimes turbulent state, Rainy Lake has an irresistible pull on paddlers. Canoers and kayakers venture into this huge body of international water for things it offers that can't be found elsewhere in Voyageurs National Park.

For one thing, the size of Rainy Lake is inviting. It covers more than 350 square miles, has 2500 miles of shoreline, and is broken up by 1600 islands, of which 651 lie inside the park. Even though most of the lake lies in Canada, it is the largest body of water within Voyageurs. In the Rainy Lake area, there are places where you can see farther than you can paddle to in a day.

The shoreline scenery is intriguing. It is a rugged blend of rock outcroppings, craggy lake shore, steep bluffs broken up by narrow bays, and islands that shelter paddlers from much of the open water of the lake. It is along the American side, from Kempton Channel to Anderson Bay, where most visitors stand in awe of Voyageurs' beauty and then leave, cherishing it as a very special part of the Border Lakes region.

But beyond its size, its scenery, and even the good fishing for walleye, northern pike, and smallmouth bass, Rainy Lake represents the wild nature of the park for many visitors. Any time spent paddling the lake usually results in at least one afternoon huddling on its shore waiting for the waves to subside. The angle of the lake, predominantly from northwest to southeast, allows northern winds to blow the length of it and create a surf that at times can easily overwhelm small boats. Waves breaking at 2 to 3 feet are common, 4-footers are not unusual, and many local residents will tell you stories of 8-foot swells crashing along the shore.

Rainy Lake's rough disposition of wind and waves is combined with its wide expanse of open water and an uncrowded and isolated nature. The result is a

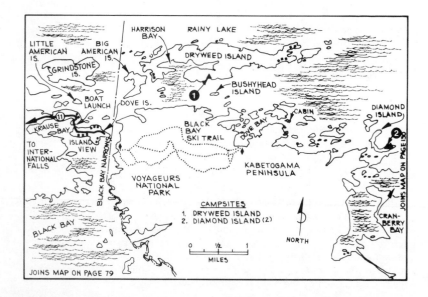

challenging paddle that will strain the shoulders but soothe the mind. In this section of Voyageurs National Park you can witness Rainy's savage nature and then portage into the Kabetogama Peninsula to satisfy a craving for wilderness adventure.

Those who plan to paddle long stretches of Rainy should allow an extra day, along with a spare paddle. The sudden change in weather that often precedes high winds will force an occasional unscheduled rest period. You should protect yourself by staying close to the shore and watching for dark storm clouds. These black clouds are the telltale signs of approaching thunderstorms and cold fronts, which can sweep in with incredible speed.

Island View is the only access point into the lower half of Rainy Lake that you can reach by car. You can also reach portions of the lake by portaging Gold Portage into Black Bay (see chapter 8) or doing the same at Kettle Falls (see chapter 9).

ISLAND VIEW TO SOLDIER POINT

Distance: 16.5 miles
Portages: 2
Longest portage: 0.75 mile
Paddling time: 2 days

The public boat ramp at Island View is located right before the bridge to Dove Island on State Highway 11 and provides parking space for vehicles left overnight. From the wooden bridge look to the northeast for a green reflector sign at the southern end of Big American Island. Use this to guide yourself into the channel formed by Dryweed Island to the north and the Kabetogama Peninsula on the south. This section can be confusing with its many channels and islands and paddlers could easily enter Black Bay thinking they were heading east into Rainy Lake.

You are now entering the Gold Mine Historic District, the stage of the 1894 gold rush to Rainy Lake. The remains of seven former mines can be found on Big American Island, Dryweed Island, Bushyhead Island, the Kabetogama Peninsula, and Little American Island. Many, like the one at the top of the rise on the southwest end of Big American Island, appear as small holes in the ground filled with rocks or water.

On Little American Island, however, both the old vertical shaft and the waste rock debris are easy to spot and to envision as a working mine. The island is situated almost 0.5 mile northeast of the public boat ramp and the mine tailings can be seen from the water along its south shore. At one time the island had numerous shafts and open mines on it, and a bunkhouse, shafthouse, headquarters building, and loading facilities were constructed to handle the miners and ore.

On a calm day you can sprint across the open stretch to the south shore of Big American Island in 15 to 20 minutes, but it is not uncommon for this area to be choppy. In this case you will need to take a longer route along the shoreline and across the northern entrance of Black Bay Narrows. Just beyond Big American Island to the east are three smaller islands, the largest of which has a cabin on it. After paddling past these you will be able to see the mouth of Harrison Bay on Dryweed Island to the north.

A stone island in Rainy Lake

Situated in the entrance of Harrison Bay is a round island and 0.3 mile to the east of the T-shaped bay, along the south shore of Dryweed Island, is the floating dock that marks a VNP campsite.

DRYWEED ISLAND CAMPSITE: The campsite is situated in a small cove on the south side of Dryweed Island and provides a fire ring, table, and pit toilet. Behind the campsite is a rocky bluff that offers good views of the channel, nearby Bushyhead Island, and the Kabetogama Peninsula.

Almost due south of the campsite in the middle of the channel is Bushyhead Island, named after "Bushy Head" Johnson who was in charge of a mine on it. Johnson kept the shaft in operation for two years, a rare feat during the Rainy Lake Gold Rush; the only other mine to last longer than a year was Little American. Continue south from the island and you will reach a cove on the mainland with a small island located on its northeast corner. The east side of the cove is formed by a long peninsula that separates it from Dove Bay.

The bay, which extends 0.7 mile to the southwest, has a dozen islands scattered in and around it and offers calm water during rough weather. Much of Dove Bay's backside is composed of marsh, making it an ideal place to spot deer feeding along the shoreline in early morning or at dusk. After paddling past the first line of islands into it, look to the south for the VNP sign that marks the east end of the Black Bay Ski Trail (see chapter 13).

Dove Bay's east side is formed by a 0.5-mile-long peninsula extending north, with a large island just above it. The channel that the peninsula and island form leads out of the bay and past some cabins to the east. From here it is 1.5 miles due east to Diamond Island through a maze of over 30 islands and islets of various sizes and shapes.

If you drop south and follow the shoreline of the Kabetogama Peninsula you will quickly see the sandy marsh area that makes up the west side of Diamond Island, still a mile away. At one point you will pass a narrow inlet with an island blocking its entrance and then paddle along a small peninsula extending east. On the tip of the peninsula are an old wooden dock and the stone foundation of a building. From here it is only a few strokes to Diamond Island's west side.

Beyond portaging across the short neck of the island, the only way to reach Diamond's east side where the VNP campsites are located is to paddle toward its north end. The waterways off its south side have long been filled in by marsh grass, and the channel to the south leads only to extensive marsh areas. After rounding the horseshoe-shaped island's north end you will pass a small, sandy cove that is often used as a camping spot. The bay that the island is curved around appears next, and on its south side are the VNP campsites.

DIAMOND ISLAND CAMPSITES: Two campsites are located here, one on each side of a sandy strip located toward Diamond's southeast tip. Each site provides a fire ring and a table. They share the single open pit toilet situated between them. The site to the east has a superb view of Rainy Lake and Cranberry Island, but tends to get windy at times. Another scenic spot can be reached by cutting across Diamond Island south of the campsites to view an extensive stretch of marsh grass and a beaver lodge.

It is only a few strokes east from the campsite to the southern tip of Diamond Island, where a channel south leads to the marsh grass behind it. Due east is a pair of small islands with the remains of an old vehicle sitting on the southern one. Pass through the gap between them and swing south to enter the channel to Cranberry Bay. Much of the channel is formed by a large unnamed island to the west and Arden Island to the east.

The channel puts you in Cranberry Bay, across from a large round boulder left in its present location by glaciers 10,000 years ago. Cranberry Bay, an entry point into the Chain of Lakes (see chapter 10), lies to the southwest. Paddle east and you will depart the large bay and swing into Alder Creek Bay after passing several islets located in its mouth. Much of the shoreline of Alder Creek is marsh grass that attracts deer in the early morning or at dusk and an occasional fisherman seeking a battle with a large northern pike.

Two long islands running from north to south separate Alder Creek Bay from Rainy Lake, and the channel between them is an avenue to the open water of the large lake. On the northern end of the island to the west is the fish camp that was built and used by Harry Oveson, one of the last commercial fishermen to work within the park. East of the fish camp is the northern tip of the second island and from there you can see the entrance of Lost Bay.

The long bay stretches 2 miles to the east but because of its angle offers little protection in its upper half from stormy northwest winds. Paddle 0.5 mile inside and look to the north shore for the VNP sign to Lost Bay Campsite.

LOST BAY CAMPSITE: The site is located at the base of an L-shaped inlet and provides a table, fire ring, open pit toilet, and space for a number of tents.

The table and fire ring face west on the sandy shoreline of Lost Bay, and a dock lies in the protection of the inlet.

The backside of Lost Bay is composed of numerous islands and extensive marsh areas, making it a sanctuary for waterfowl, herons, and eagles, as well as a few anglers trying their luck for walleye and northern pike. Along the south shore is a large cove with seven islands and islets sitting in its entrance. Paddle into the cove and look to its east side for the route to Saginaw Bay.

LOST BAY TO SAGINAW BAY PORTAGE (Rating—extremely difficult; distance—0.75 mile): During the winter this route is a quick, easy way for skiers and snowmobilers to reduce their traveling time and avoid dangerous ice on their way to Saginaw Bay. But during the summer it would be an extremely difficult, almost impossible portage trip for paddlers. The entire route follows marsh area and you will be in knee-deep water from the moment you step out of your boat. Both ends are marked.

Someday the VNP might construct a summer portage from Lost Bay to Saginaw Bay, for there is a great need for one. Until then paddlers have to cautiously round Soldier Point. Do not try this stretch in anything less than ideal conditions. By the time northwest winds reach Soldier Point and Brule Narrows they have gathered momentum on the open water and are driving the surf hard into this corner of the lake.

The increasing wave action is felt in the entrance of Lost Bay and even more so when you head north of the bay in the channel formed by two small islands and Harbor Island. Once past Harbor Island and heading east you will be in Rainy Lake and subject to whatever is sweeping across the open water. For the next 2.6 miles, until you enter Brule Narrows, there are only a dozen small islands to paddle behind for protection. They are not enough to ensure a safe trip during rough weather.

There are two bays you can dip into for protection along this stretch. The first is 0.5 mile from Harbor Island and has several islands in its entrance. The shoreline from here heads east for 0.5 mile, then swings south toward the second

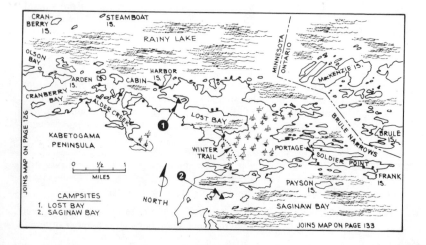

CRANBERRY IS. STEAMBOAT IS.

RAINY LAKE

OLSON BAY

HARBOR

ARDEN IS. CABIN IS.

CRANBERRY BAY

MINNESOTA ONTARIO

MacKENZIE IS.

ALDER CREEK

LOST BAY

BRULE NARROWS

BRULE IS.

KABETOGAMA PENINSULA

JOINS MAP ON PAGE 126

0   ½   1
MILES

WINTER TRAIL

PORTAGE

SOLDIER POINT

FRANK IS.

PAYSON IS.

NORTH

CAMPSITES
1. LOST BAY
2. SAGINAW BAY

SAGINAW BAY

JOINS MAP ON PAGE 133

Colony of cormorants at Rainy Lake

bay, which offers calm water during even the roughest storms. The bay extends 0.25 mile to the west and on its north shore has the remains of two old cabins. This is the spot to stay put or even spend the night if the lake is kicking up, since the next mile to Brule Narrows is the roughest section to paddle.

From the small bay the shoreline heads east again as you follow the north side of a long, narrow peninsula. Three narrow islands parallel the peninsula at its tip and are the key to rounding it safely in canoes and kayaks. Still at times the channel they form and the gaps between the islands can make for choppy conditions. Upon reaching the spot where both the third island and the peninsula end, you head south into the large bay whose south shore is formed by Soldier Point.

This bay is often a sigh of relief for paddlers and motorboaters alike as it offers protection from wind and waves. You can actually sit on the edge of the bay in calm water and watch the waves breaking 100 yards in front of you in Brule Narrows. The bay is formed to the south by the 2.3-mile-long Soldier Point, named after Canadian Colonel Garnet Wolseley and his expeditionary force of 1400 men who passed through the narrows in 1870 to suppress the rebellion by Métis leader Louis Riel. You see the east tip of the point almost as soon as you enter Brule Narrows, and if the water is calm it can be a very scenic paddle.

If not, then it is best to stay inside the bay and paddle south through its maze of islands, several of them long and narrow. It is a little over 0.5 mile from the north side of the bay to the largest island to the south, which runs parallel to Soldier Point. At the west end of the island there is an islet with a beaver lodge on it. This is the starting point for a quick portage route into Saginaw Bay.

SAGINAW BAY PORTAGE (Rating—moderate; distance—0.2 mile): From the beaver lodge, paddle due south to Soldier Point. From this point it is a straight hike south across the peninsula along a route that climbs a slight ridge and then descends to a cove off Saginaw Bay. There is marsh grass in the cove, but nothing that canoers and kayakers can't paddle through.

SOLDIER POINT TO KETTLE FALLS

Distance: 26 miles
Portages: 3
Longest portage: 1.2 miles
Paddling time: 2–3 days

After rounding the eastern tip of Soldier Point you can head west into Saginaw Bay, an area of calm water and usually few if any boats. A natural channel is formed by Soldier Point's south shore and a line of islands beginning with Frank Island. The broken channel extends almost 2 miles due west. If you are paddling in early morning, keep an eye out for deer feeding along the shores of Soldier Point and the various islands.

After passing the entrance of a cove that extends 0.5 mile west at the base of Soldier Point, the main shoreline begins to swing southwest and leads you deep into the bay. This portion of Saginaw Bay is a beautiful section of the park, its usually calm water is broken up by a dozen or so islands and islets. The three largest form a line in the back of the bay, and the one in the middle has a VNP campsite on it.

SAGINAW BAY CAMPSITE: Located on the western end of an unnamed island deep in Saginaw Bay, this scenic site offers a table, fire ring, covered pit toilet, and a dock. There is space for a number of tents.

North from the campsite dock is the cove where the snowmobile portage from Lost Bay terminates. Much of the cove is filled with marsh grass and lends itself well to wildlife sightings of a variety of waterfowl and deer.

South from the campsite is a cove, with a larger one just west of it. Round the head that forms the east side of the smaller cove, and you will come to a sandy cove on the other side. From here it is a 0.75-mile paddle to Marion Bay, a large body of water that features three narrow inlets and two peninsulas on its backside. The east side of Marion Bay is formed by a large head and as you round it you will flow into a wide channel formed by two islands to the north, the smaller of which is Duckfoot Island. From the channel it is a straight paddle to Little Finlander Island and the VNP campsite on it.

LITTLE FINLANDER ISLAND CAMPSITE: The campsite is located on the east side of the island along a protected channel formed by Finlander Island to the east. It features a sandy strip or beach—depending on the water level— that is ideal for a quick dip into chilly Rainy Lake. There is also a fire ring, pit toilet, and a table where you can sit and view both sides of the island's narrow north end.

Beginning with Little Finlander Island and continuing right into Kempton Channel, paddlers and motorboaters alike will find a protective system of channels and islands that is very safe even when a northwest wind is blowing. After dropping south through the channel between the two Finlander islands you arrive at a narrow inlet that is blocked by a large island. The gap at the west end of the island is almost closed by marsh grass, but paddlers can still squeeze through.

The long inlet features marsh vegetation and usually an abundance of waterfowl enjoying its calm conditions. The east gap is wide, and beyond the island it is a 0.5-mile paddle to Nelson Island and the narrow channel it forms with the south shore of Rainy Lake. Once inside you quickly come to a T-shaped junction, with one channel heading northeast out to Rainy Lake and the other departing south for 0.5 mile into Hitchcock Bay.

Beginning with the southern channel and ending at Anderson Bay is a section of the park that most visitors come to remember and cherish long after they leave. The beauty comes from the mixture of narrow channels, steep shoreline bluffs, and towering pines broken up by smooth slabs of granite—all set against the backdrop of Rainy Lake's wide expanse of water. The channel into Hitchcock Bay, only 150 yards at its widest point, snakes its way south until it suddenly breaks out into the open water of the bay.

The west end of Hitchcock Bay is a narrow inlet where the shoreline of the Kabetogama Peninsula swings southeast. Once you are past the inlet Hitchcock Island comes into view straight ahead, with the larger Kawawia Island situated northeast of it. The roundish island north of Kawawia, which appears to be sitting in the middle of a channel, is Norway Island.

Hitchcock Island is small and can be distinguished by a stone fireplace and chimney, the remains of an old cabin, on its west end. Occasionally someone will camp here but most people will paddle south around it and then swing to the northwest for the VNP campsite on Kawawia Island.

KAWAWIA ISLAND CAMPSITE: The campsite is located on a small point on the southwest corner of the large island. There is a dock on the east side of the point and a table and fire ring facing the west side. The site also contains a pit toilet and ample space for tents.

Departing east from the campsite, you follow the south side of Kawawia Island and come to a channel that heads northeast to Rainy Lake and Big Island's north shore. Straight ahead is Kempton Channel, the narrow, glacially carved waterway that extends 2.2 miles along the south shore of Big Island. Halfway along this calm, scenic waterway a long, narrow inlet extends 0.75 mile east into Big Island, almost cutting the island in half. The west side of the inlet's entrance is a traditional camping spot.

At the southeast corner of Big Island Kempton Channel opens up to Kempton

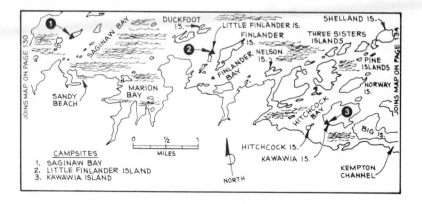

Bay. Due south along the shore of Kabetogama Peninsula is a large cove that narrows down to a small slip where a stream empties into it. This is the starting point for the northern route into Shoepack Lake (see chapter 10).

BIG ISLAND: The island is aptly named, since it is the largest one along this stretch of Rainy Lake's American shoreline. It has a highly irregular shoreline, a few cabins along its north shore, and some scenic bluffs on its east side and northeast corner. The island's east shore is a series of small points. The first one appears only a few strokes after rounding the southeast corner and is the site of an old campsite, now overgrown with brush. A little farther north is the start of a massive stretch of bare rock shoreline and bluffs that continues past Stoffels Point.

Stoffels Point is a small peninsula that extends toward Blueberry Island; situated south of it is an island with a sandy cove at its north end. Older maps have a cabin on the north end, but the structure is gone and today the cove is a beautiful camping spot with a sandy beach and a scenic view of the nearby islands and Rainy Lake. In the middle of the island are some huge rock slabs where you could lie to enjoy the afternoon sun.

North of Stoffels Point is a small bay whose shoreline is broken up by several small points of land. A boat can be landed in the tiny cove between the second and third point. The VNP campsite is situated above the cove's shoreline.

BIG ISLAND CAMPSITE: The campsite requires a second look to find it and some visitors may miss it altogether. That's a shame because it is situated on a huge rock above the shoreline for a scenic view of Rainy Lake. Along with a table, fire ring, and open pit toilet, the site provides access to a sandy beach just north of it in the bay.

Those who continue around Stoffels Point to the north shore of Big Island should be prepared for considerably rougher water than they experienced in Kempton Channel or Kempton Bay. From the VNP campsite you round a head of land into the open lake, but can immediately dip into the larger bay on its west side. This bay on the northeast corner of the island is a quiet spot, with steep bluffs along its east side and a few camping spots deep inside and on the west

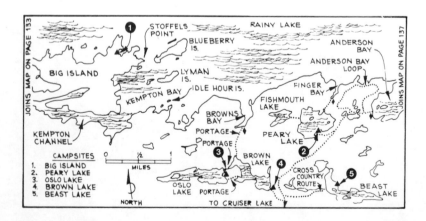

Anderson Bay off Rainy Lake, as seen from the Anderson Bay Loop Trail

shore. But there is no official VNP campsite, even though one is shown on many maps.

Kempton Bay lies to the east of the southeast corner of Big Island, bordered to the north by Lyman Island. Due south along the Kabetogama Peninsula is Idle Hour Island. Just east of Idle Hour is the entrance of a small bay with several islands in it. From the east side of the bay it is a 0.5-mile paddle along the shoreline to Browns Bay.

Browns Bay has several cabins on an L-shaped peninsula along its east side, but if you're trying to avoid all signs of human habitation, just paddle to the back of the bay and the marker for the 0.5-mile portage to Brown Lake. From this inland lake it is possible to reach several other isolated lakes and even return to Rainy Lake by way of Peary Lake (see chapter 10).

It is a 1.2-mile paddle from Browns Bay to Finger Bay along an unbroken shoreline, with no islands to protect paddlers from Rainy Lake's sudden whims. Finger Bay is 0.5 mile wide at its entrance but quickly narrows down to an inlet less than 50 yards wide. The 0.25-mile portage to Peary Lake begins at the scenic back of Finger Bay (see chapter 10).

The shoreline east of Finger Bay continues to become steeper and more rugged for the next 0.75 mile and is marked by varying pitches of smooth granite. You round one last narrow point and then are able to swing southwest into Anderson Bay.

ANDERSON BAY: Easily the most photographed section of Voyageurs National Park, Anderson Bay is a natural gem. From the low perch of a kayak or canoe in the middle of the bay, you stare at a stunning series of rounded, bare rock cliffs, polished smooth by glaciers 10,000 years ago. The bluffs rising abruptly 80 feet from the water and the sprinkling of rocky islands give the bay that special North Woods mystique.

Island in Rainy Lake

For those lucky enough to be on hand for a sunset on a clear day, Anderson Bay has another added feature. The bay is angled in such a way that it captures the last rays of the setting sun and for 20 to 30 minutes the water, cliffs, and islands glow in shades of yellow, burnt orange, and red.

In the back of the bay is a shoreline of smooth rock, with a large VNP sign marking the north end of the Cruiser Lake Trail. The first part of the trail is the Anderson Bay Loop, a 2.5-mile foottrail that leads to spectacular views of both the bay and Rainy Lake from high points on the surrounding bluffs (see chapter 12). Even if you don't have any desire to hike the Cruiser Lake Trail, you should still beach the boat and spend a couple of hours on the Anderson Bay Loop.

Camping inside the bay is difficult, since the granite shoreline and rocky islands make it difficult to find a spot to pitch a tent. The nearest VNP campsite is at Peary Lake, a 1.8-mile hike south along the Cruiser Lake Trail. Virgin Island Campsites are a 2.3-mile paddle to the east.

The water is well protected from northwest winds as you paddle out of Anderson Bay east from the Cruiser Lake Trailhead. After passing a pair of islands deep in the bay, you arrive at a chain of several more that form a broken channel just east of Anderson Bay's entrance. Beyond the third and largest island of the chain, a sandy beach with camping possibilities lies to the south on the Kabetogama Peninsula. This is followed by another island and a roundish peninsula. Once through the gap between the two, you can swing to the east and head straight for Virgin Island, which has three VNP campsites on its southern end.

VIRGIN ISLAND CAMPSITES: The entire west shore of Virgin Island—a very scenic spot—has a view of Anderson Bay's entrance and the rocky islands that surround it. You can hike along the bluffs on the west side to a sandy cove halfway up the island. The cove offers places to swim and more camping possibilities. The site features three tables, two fire rings, and a covered pit toilet as well as a dock and a sandy strip for beaching a boat.

Due south from the campsites is the trailhead for isolated Ryan Lake and its shoreline campsite. The trail runs 1.1 miles south, ending at the campsite, but can be shortened to 0.4 mile if you are portaging a boat in (see chapter 13).

From the trailhead on Rainy Lake you head east for 0.5 mile and then begin rounding a substantial head with two cabins on its east shore. The shoreline curves in a southeast direction and arrives at a large peninsula connected to the mainland by a 5-yard strip of sand and grass. Paddlers can drag their boats over the strip to save a few strokes.

On the other side is a well-protected cove with a stream emptying into it. A tote road located next to the stream wanders back a short way to the remains of some old cabins, and on topographical maps it is shown continuing west to Ryan Lake and south to Mica Bay. It is extremely difficult, however, to find the path after the first 200 yards.

From the back of the cove you paddle northeast and depart through its narrow entrance, passing the small mouth of another cove that parallels it. If a northwest wind is blowing, there will be a brief stretch of choppy water from the entrance of the cove until you dip into the protective channel formed by Sand Bay Island. Keep an eye on the shoreline of the Kabetogama Peninsula as you pass the east end of Sand Bay Island for the first of two VNP campsites.

LOGGING CAMP CAMPSITE: Located on a shallow cove just east of Sand Bay Island, the site provides a pit toilet, table, and fire ring, and near the VNP sign is a sandy strip where you can beach a boat.

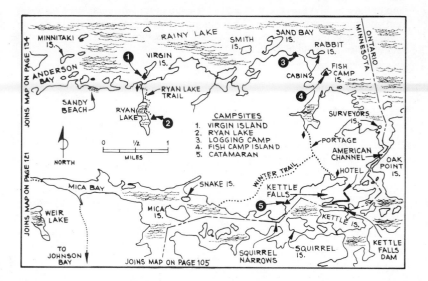

FISH CAMP ISLAND CAMPSITE: From Logging Camp Campsite the shoreline swings south and you paddle past Rabbit Island straight for the smaller Fish Camp Island, marked with an NPS sign. The campsite, located on the northwest point of the island, provides a table, fire ring, open pit toilet, and a strip of sand near the VNP sign where you can pull a boat up. The spot has a nice view of Kabetogama Peninsula and Rabbit Island to the northwest and on a clear evening is a good place to watch the sunset.

The bay south of Fish Camp Island extends for almost a mile, with marsh grass along much of its west shore and back side. There is a lone cabin near the entrance on the east shore, and at the very back is a snowmobile sign to the portage for Namakan Lake.

RAINY LAKE–NAMAKAN LAKE PORTAGE (Rating— extremely difficult; distance—1.2 miles): From the portage marker you head due south through the tall grass, following the line of young trees to the west. There seems to be no trail here, but once in the forest you will see a definite trail that continues south along a level, dry course. After 0.4 mile it comes to a large beaver pond with a trail marker in the middle. To the west is more extensive marsh area stretching to Mica Bay. The trail resumes straight ahead, on the other side of the pond.

Here paddlers must reload their boats to cross the pond and then continue with the portage. On the other side the trail follows a fairly level course between two ridges but can be extremely wet, if not completely impassable, during the summer. It continues for 0.8 mile, curving slightly to the east where it comes out at a small cove that is the most northern point of Namakan Lake and a short paddle away from Kettle Falls.

This is an extremely tough portage to undertake because of its length and wetness during the summer. It is far easier to paddle the American Channel and portage over at the Kettle Falls dam. To do this depart east from the entrance of the bay on Rainy Lake and round a large head that features several coves and rocky bluffs. After you pass three small coves side by side you will spot a Canadian island to the east and Surveyors Island to the south. From the small American island you can see the entrance of the American Channel. Kettle Falls is a mile south. The channel is narrow and paddlers should be alert for motorboaters, who will also be using it.

(Opposite) Campsite at Quill Lake

PART THREE

VOYAGEURS ON FOOT: HIKING, SKIING, AND SNOWSHOEING

12   CRUISER LAKE TRAIL SYSTEM

It had all the drama of Henry Stanley meeting Dr. Livingston in the middle of Africa: Deep in the middle of Voyageurs National Park two solitary hikers moved toward each other along an old logging trail.

On the four outside lakes that form the boundaries of the park there might have been 300 boats and canoes filled with fishermen, campers, and paddlers. But isolated Kabetogama Peninsula probably had fewer than a dozen backpackers exploring its interior and two of us had selected the same overgrown logging trail.

We saw each other long before we met. The trail was easy to follow but difficult to hike. It was built during the 1920s for pulling log sleds over the frozen ground during the winter, not for hiking on during the summer. Much of it was layers of muskeg floating on top of 6 to 18 inches of stagnant water and forcing you to hike with wobbly legs. It was like making your way across the showroom of a waterbed store by walking on the merchandise.

When we finally approached each other, we stopped only momentarily, nodded to each other, and he asked, "A nice day for slogging, isn't it?"

Couldn't be better. No word describes cross-country travel in Voyageurs National Park better than slogging. Throughout much of the park you don't hike, you slog. You wear 14-inch rubber boots, you bounce along floating muskeg, you tiptoe across a beaver dam that has turned 0.5 mile of logging trail into a pond.

Fawn eating shrubs.

And suddenly you are confronted by a pair of bucks feeding on young aspen trees, a 300-pound black bear digging up roots, or maybe even a moose making its way through knee-deep water—but rarely by another hiker.

You don't have to slog, however, to achieve wilderness solitude or spot wildlife in the middle of the Kabetogama Peninsula. In addition to the dozens of old tote roads that crisscross the park, the NPS has developed 32 miles of hiking trails. Most of them center around the Cruiser Lake Trail system, which traverses the peninsula from Lost Bay on the south shore to Anderson Bay off Rainy Lake. These trails were built with summer hikers in mind. Unlike the tote roads, they are marked, easy to follow, and planked when they cross swamps or ponds.

The Cruiser Lake system connects eight campsites and touches the shores of seven inland lakes. Hikers can combine the various trails for a relaxing four- or five-day backpacking trip, beginning and ending at Lost Bay and climaxing at Anderson Bay on the north shore.

One itinerary for covering the Cruiser Lake Trail with the least amount of backtracking is to begin by hiking from Lost Bay to Jorgens Lake (see chapter 10) the first night and then following the unmaintained Overlook Trail the second day and camping at Cruiser Lake. The third day would include camping at Brown Lake or Peary Lake and continuing in the afternoon to view Anderson Bay. The fourth day would be used to return by way of the Cruiser Lake Trail and camp at Agnes Lake. This hike would add up to a total of 30 miles.

LOST BAY TO ANDERSON BAY

Distance: 9.1 miles
Hiking time: 5–8 hours
High point: 1330 feet
Rating: moderate

The trail begins at the east end of Lost Bay at a large VNP sign and dock and immediately ascends a predominantly aspen and birch forest, reaching a junction in 0.2 mile. The spur to the northwest leads to the unmaintained Overlook Trail and Overlook viewpoint 1.6 miles away.

The Cruiser Lake Trail is the northeast fork, which climbs along a rocky ridge for 0.5 mile and then opens up to a view of Agnes Lake to the east. Keep an eye out for the rock cairns on the ridge and they will lead you to a marked spur that descends to the lake.

AGNES LAKE AND CAMPSITE: The scenic campsite, which sits on the west side of the lake, provides a fire ring, table, and covered pit toilet. Campers can revel in the blueberries on the ridge behind it beginning in mid-July, and anglers can scramble along the west shore in an effort to hook a northern pike. The lake measures 0.5 mile in length and borders marsh areas at both its north and south ends, making it difficult to circle on foot.

From the spur to Agnes Lake the trail levels out through a predominantly pine forest before dropping and skirting a large marsh area where deer can often be spotted in the early morning or at dusk. The trail ascends a ridge and opens on a scenic view of the wetlands to the east and Agnes Lake off in the distance to the south. It follows the ridge, with more views of the marsh area, until it descends to a junction. The side trail is the Agnes Lake Cutoff, which extends 0.5 mile west to

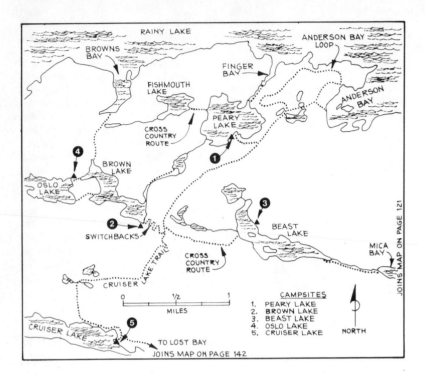

the Overlook Trail. From this point Cruiser Lake lies 3.5 miles to the north and Lost Bay is 1 mile south along the Cruiser Lake Trail.

Just past the junction the trail crosses a stream that has been choked off by a beaver dam, then swings around the pond to the east before it begins to ascend through a sparse stand of aspen and birch. Here hikers will find extensive blueberry patches.

A half-mile from the junction the trail passes an unnamed lake with extensive marsh along its shores. There is a smooth slab of granite and an excellent view of the area as the trail passes due west of the lake. From the clearing the trail enters a thick forest for 0.5 mile before breaking out at another beaver pond. Just before crossing the stream you come to a junction between the north end of the Overlook Trail and the Cruiser Lake Trail. The Overlook heads west and will reach the viewpoint in 1.4 miles and return to the Lost Bay Trailhead in 3.2 miles. Straight ahead is Cruiser Lake campsite, 2.3 miles away.

From the junction the trail crosses the stream north and then ascends gradually for the next 0.5 mile until it peaks at a rocky crest of a ridge. At this point hikers are rewarded with views of the rolling, forested terrain to the south before the trail continues as a series of rock cairns over the ridge top. Blueberries and strawberries grow profusely along the open ridge, so hikers should keep one eye on cairns and the other out for the black butt of a bear feasting on berries.

Waterfall off Cruiser Lake Trail

The trail dips back to the forest for 0.4 mile and then returns to the ridge crest and passes a small cave formed by an overhanging slab of rock. Again it dips into forest to cross a stream and then climbs to another rock bluff. After one more drop into forest terrain the trail emerges on a ridge with a view of a beaver pond to the north. Soon a second beaver pond to the south comes into view, as the trail crosses a ridge between the two bodies of water.

The trail begins to descend toward the shoreline of the southern pond and bottoms out at a stream. Upon closer inspection the stream reveals a beautiful waterfall that cascades 10 feet over bare rock into a deep pool. Cruiser Lake campsite is less than a mile northwest from the waterfalls over the steadily climbing trail. At one point there is another glimpse of the northern pond as the trail circles around it. Eventually the trail peaks out on a ridge, follows it for a spell, and then begins to descend to the Cruiser Lake Campsite junction.

A spur descends off the ridge to an island in the east end of the lake. You can walk to the VNP campsite across a wooden boardwalk that connects the shoreline to the island.

CRUISER LAKE AND CAMPSITE: The cold, crystal clear water in 1.25-mile-long Cruiser Lake is thought by many to be the purest in the park. The lake is 0.25 mile wide, has a maximum depth of 91 feet, and is renowned for its population of lake trout. Before warm weather sends them to the deeper sections of the lake, the large fish can be caught in early June by surface trolling, even from the shoreline.

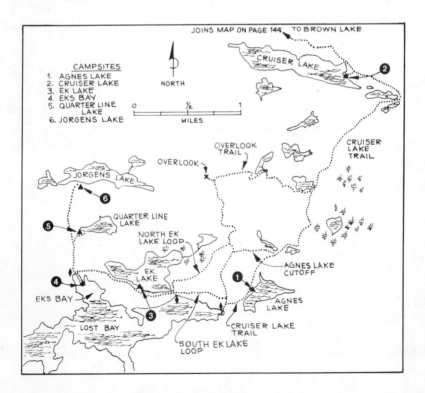

Brown Lake from the Cruiser Lake Trail

At one time the campsite sat on the northern shore of the lake, but was moved recently to a location farther from the main trail. Today it sits on a small island at the east end of the lake and from its table you can see the entire length of Cruiser Lake. There is also a fire ring and a tent pad, since level space is scarce. A pit toilet is located back across the boardwalk on the mainland.

The trail departs from the spur to Cruiser Lake Campsite and follows the north shore of the lake, rising and dipping with the grassy bluffs along the shoreline. This is a haven for berry lovers—the open bluffs offer blueberry and strawberry patches that ripen early in the summer. In 0.3 mile from the spur the trail passes the old location of the Cruiser Lake Campsite and then swings sharply north for Brown Lake.

The trail follows a level course through forested terrain until it breaks out at a beaver pond where, as a posted sign indicates, you cross the pond by following an old, grass-covered beaver dam. The ancient structure has since been replaced by a newer one just to the east and beyond it is a large pond and open area. From either Brown Lake or Cruiser Lake this spot is a pleasant hike at dusk to view a variety of wildlife.

The trail swings to the east and follows the pond for a short distance before heading north and making a gradual climb for the next 0.3 mile. Eventually it breaks out on top of a ridge where the trees and brush are thin and hikers have to keep an eye out for rock cairns. The trail follows the ridge for almost 0.5 mile, mostly over bare rock, until it drops sharply into a wet area.

The small swamp has been planked and the trail departs from it by ascending the ridge on the other side. Once at the top it arrives at a junction with the spur to Brown Lake. The campsite lies 0.5 mile to the west, Anderson Bay is 3.3 miles north, and Cruiser Lake Campsite is 1.6 miles to the south.

The spur to Brown Lake follows the rocky ridge west for the first 100 yards until it comes to a spectacular view of the lake from above. From this point it curves north and begins a very sharp descent straight to the campsite on the east end (see chapter 10 for a description of the lake and campsite). Those portaging a boat in from Beast Lake have to use extreme caution when descending this steep trail.

The Cruiser Lake Trail remains on the ridge past the junction to Brown Lake and then begins a gradual descent before dropping more steeply as it bottoms out in a young aspen and birch forest. You immediately begin to climb again and will soon pass through a clearing of rock and scrub. Scramble to the east here for an excellent view of an old beaver pond slowly being reclaimed by marsh grass and shrubs. The gap at the east end of the pond is the stream that eventually flows into Beast Lake.

For the next 1.4 miles the trail dips and climbs over the backs of three major ridges, with no landmarks to view except the trees around you. There are a number of turns in the trail on solid rock, but there always seems to be a rock cairn when you need one. This section is dry throughout.

Those hikers with a sharp eye might catch a glimpse of Rainy Lake 0.8 mile past the view of the beaver pond or 0.6 mile before the posted Peary Lake junction. The sign may say 0.1 mile to the campsite, but it's more like 0.3 mile.

The spur to the lake consists of a steady drop toward the water before it levels out and swings to the southwest to circle the shoreline. It ends at a small point of land in the southeast corner. The campsite is cramped but Peary is a scenic and interesting lake for an overnight stay (see chapter 10 for description).

The section of the Cruiser Lake Trail from Peary Lake to Anderson Bay is the most scenic of the entire route. It departs from the junction and remains on the ridge to hug the east shore of Peary Lake. With every bend in the trail, the view of the round lake gets a little better. The trail dips once on this ridge, returns to its former height, and then climbs a little higher on an immense rock bluff. Here hikers are rewarded with a grand panorama of the entire lake from north to south.

The trail departs from the bluff and descends into forest, then breaks out of the trees at a pair of beaver ponds and dams. An old wooden bridge helps you cross the ponds from where the trail curves east around one and then swings north for a short spell to arrive at a junction with the Anderson Bay Loop Trail. The fork to the northwest leads around the loop and reaches the bay 2.5 miles away. The fork to the northeast is the other end of the loop. It leads to the bay off a spur 0.4 mile from the loop junction. Peary Lake lies 1.1 miles to the south, Brown Lake 3.4 miles, and Cruiser Lake 4.2 miles.

From the junction the trail descends sharply and crosses an arm of the beaver pond that was seen earlier before reentering forest and arriving at the spur to Anderson Bay shoreline. The 0.2-mile spur takes you right to water's edge at beautiful Anderson Bay. It descends slightly and arrives at a large milepost

Anderson Bay as seen from the Anderson Bay Loop Trail

pointing out that Peary Lake lies 1.5 miles to the south, Brown Lake 3.8 miles, and Cruiser Lake 4.6 miles.

ANDERSON BAY LOOP

Distance: 2.9 miles (round trip from bay shore)
Hiking time: 2–3 hours
High point: 1180 feet
Rating: easy

You could easily hike the entire loop in an hour if you hustled. But the scenery is spectacular along this trail and hikers should plan to spend the better part of an afternoon or morning to allow time to sit on the high bluffs and absorb it all. By hiking the loop in a clockwise manner, you will be saving the best—the overall view of Anderson Bay—for the grand finale to the trip.

Hike the 0.2-mile spur to the main trail and take the fork to the south. From here the trail quickly crosses an arm of a beaver pond and then climbs up and over a ridge toward another pond when it arrives at a junction. To the south is the rest of the Cruiser Lake Trail, with Peary Lake 1.1 miles away.

Follow the trail that heads west. It begins by climbing and then peaks out and gradually descends around a beaver pond where the Cruiser Lake Trail crosses to the south by means of a wooden bridge. Toward the west end of the pond the trail climbs a rock bluff to a scenic view of the beaver's handiwork.

From here the trail swings north and traverses the back of a ridge for the next 0.8 mile. There is a fair amount of up and down hiking, and twice the trail breaks out on a bare rock crest. The first open ridge features extensive blueberry and strawberry patches; the second, round boulders that the glaciers deposited 10,000 years ago.

The trail departs from the second crest and begins a gradual descent from which it breaks out on a bluff overlooking a small cove and Rainy Lake in the distance. The trail swings east and follows the lake shore, offering occasional glimpses of Rainy Lake. The last one comes on a roundish rock bluff where you can sit and view the large lake from Brule Narrows and Soldier Point in the west to Stokes Bay in the east. This scene is breathtaking on a clear day, but it is also impressive on a windy day when the large waves and swells smash along the rocky shore, displaying Rainy Lake's formidable power.

The trail departs the bluff and swings south, crosses through a forest area, and then breaks out on another rock bluff with Anderson Bay stretching out below. This is a magnificent sight, with the bay's high bluffs and rocky islets providing quintessential North Woods scenery. Anderson Bay is angled in such a manner that at dusk it catches the last rays of a setting sun, washing everything in oranges, yellows, and reds. You can spend hours at this spot, contemplating nature's handiwork.

From the grand view of Anderson Bay the trail leaves the shoreline bluff and moves inland following a rocky crest. It gradually descends from the ridge top through forested terrain until you reach the junction with the 0.2-mile spur to the shoreline of Anderson Bay. Continue south if you are heading back to Peary Lake Campsite spur, 1.3 miles away, or Brown Lake, 3.2 miles.

OVERLOOK TRAIL

Distance: 3 miles
Hiking time: 2–3 hours
High point: 1310 feet
Rating: moderate to difficult   Map—page 142

Although no longer maintained, the Overlook Trail can still be followed by hikers looking for a challenge and a way to avoid backtracking a segment of the Cruiser Lake Trail when crossing the Kabetogama Peninsula. It can also be combined with the southern end of the Cruiser Lake Trail for a 5.3-mile day hike out of Lost Bay. It departs west from the Cruiser Lake Trail 2.2 miles south of Cruiser Lake and rejoins the main route 0.2 mile north of the Lost Bay trailhead and dock.

The north end begins at a posted junction just south of a beaver pond and dam. From here Lost Bay trailhead lies 2.1 miles along the Cruiser Lake Trail and 3.2 miles on the Overlook Trail. The Cruiser Lake Campsite is 2.2 miles to the north.

From its north junction with the Cruiser Lake Trail, the Overlook Trail departs west by skirting the pond and passing two large slabs of stone where it is possible to walk right down to the water. Keep one eye on the pond and nearby stream, for there is often much beaver activity. The trail leaves the pond and crosses another huge stone slab where rock cairns point the way, then con-

Snowshoer with sled, moving toward Jorgens Lake (Steve Maass photo)

tinues along the rocky backbone of a ridge. Again you have to keep an eye out for the rock cairns as it is easy to get turned around.

After 0.3 mile of open ridge top the trail swings north away from the bare rock crest, but the natural inclination is to continue following the ridge. Those who do will discover an absence of rock cairns. The trail heads north through low brush that is easy to get confused in and then swings west again along another rocky ridge. Soon you will spot the end of a large beaver pond through the trees.

The trail skirts the south end of the pond and then heads west following more slabs of rock most of the way to Overlook viewpoint. Gradually the trail begins to swing to the southwest, and 1.4 miles from the Cruiser Lake Trail junction you arrive at Overlook.

The spot is 1310 feet high and earned its name from the good views of the peninsula's rolling terrain and Jorgens Lake off to the west. If there is any wind at all the point will be almost bug free and a pleasant spot for lunch or an extended break. From here Lost Bay trailhead lies 1.8 miles to the south. Those heading in the other direction still have to hike 3.6 miles to reach the Cruiser Lake Campsite.

From the scenic point the trail heads south and makes a rapid descent, passing an old beaver pond along the way. The descent is 0.75 mile long and runs through a forest of aspen, birch, and white spruce. Eventually you bottom out where a marsh area and lake lie to the west. Here the trail skirts the wetlands and then climbs another high point of 1220 feet to a junction with the Ek Lake Loop, a trail that departs west and connects Ek, Quarter Line, and Jorgens lakes with the Cruiser Lake Trail system.

The Overlook Trail departs south off the high point, crosses a planked wet area, and then climbs to another junction 0.2 mile from the last one. Here the Agnes Lake cutoff extends 0.5 mile east to the Cruiser Lake Trail, where you can head south to the campsite on the small lake. Lost Bay lies 0.7 mile to the south on the Overlook Trail.

The trail levels out for a short distance through thick pine forest before descending and crossing a planked wetland. From here the trail completes its route by climbing two more small ridges and then leveling out to the junction with the Cruiser Lake Trail immediately after passing the southern trail to the Ek Lake Loop. At this point Lost Bay trailhead and dock lie 0.2 mile to the south and the Agnes Lake cutoff lies 0.5 mile to the north along the Cruiser Lake Trail.

EK LAKE LOOP

Round trip Overlook Trail to Jorgens Lake
Distance: 6.9 miles including spurs
Hiking time: 3–4 hours
High point: 1220 feet
Rating: mild   **Map—page 142**

The Ek Lake Loop consists of two trails that depart west from the Overlook Trail and come together at the southeast corner of the lake. From here the trail follows the south shore of Ek Lake, passes its campsite, and then joins the portage trail to Quarter Line and Jorgens lakes. The loop can be used as a pleasant day hike out of Lost Bay or can be added to the Cruiser Lake Trail to extend a backpacking trip another day or two.

The southern trail of the loop begins 0.25 mile from the Lost Bay trailhead and dock, off the Overlook Trail just north of its junction with the Cruiser Lake Trail. It begins with an ascent to the west from the birch and aspen forest to a ridge where you will be traveling along a rocky crest much of the way. A good set of rock cairns keeps you on track. Those who love blueberries and strawberries will have a field day in July and August.

Gradually the trail moves to the side of the ridge and patches of Lost Bay begin to appear, until you find yourself standing at the edge where a grassy slope leads straight down to the water. This is one of the best views in the park—you can see the entire lower portion of Lost Bay, with its deep blue water and the bluffs that make up much of its shoreline.

The trail leaves the viewing point and soon comes to the junction with the northern half of the loop, a trail that departs 0.9 mile northeast to the Overlook Trail. From here the two trails become one and descend sharply off the ridge to the short portage between Ek Lake and Lost Bay, the latter only 0.1 mile to the south.

From the short portage the Ek Lake Trail heads west, where it comes to a marshy area that is crossed by a wooden walkway. The trail then ascends a ridge from which there is a steady view of the lake. The trail skirts the south shore and arrives at a rock bluff from which you can see almost all of Ek Lake. This portion lasts less than 0.5 mile before the trail drops off the ridge and arrives at the short spur to the Ek Lake Campsite.

EK LAKE AND CAMPSITE: The spur heads north 0.1 mile to the water's edge where the campsite is located. The site provides a covered pit toilet, fire ring, and a table that is no more than 5 feet from the lapping water of the lake. Tent space is limited but the view is good since the site overlooks the long cove at the west end of the lake.

The lake, which has a small islet near its west end, is 0.75 mile long and almost 0.5 mile wide. Maximum depth of the lake is 19 feet and anglers do well when fishing for northern pike, crappies, and perch.

From the campsite spur the trail ascends another ridge and follows it west along the lake, where after 0.5 mile of hiking you are again treated to views first of the lake to the northeast and then of Eks Bay to the south.

The trail then descends the ridge, crosses a planked stream, and finishes with a level walk through wooded terrain where it forms a junction with the portage trail to Quarter Line and Jorgens lakes (see chapter 10). Eks Bay lies 100 yards to the south, Quarter Line Lake Campsite is 0.6 mile to the north, and Jorgens Lake Campsite is 1 mile north (for trail descriptions see chapter 10).

NORTHERN EK LAKE LOOP (Distance—0.9 mile): The northern trail of the Ek Lake Loop departs from the junction with the southern half and sharply descends the ridge to the east end of the lake, where it comes to within 5 feet of the water. It quickly ascends another ridge and follows it east away from the lake only to sharply descend off this one and bottom out at an old marsh area that is being reclaimed by young aspen trees.

The trail climbs slightly into a growth of pine trees and then breaks out into a wet area that is crossed by planking. From here the trail curves to the west and begins to climb before curving back to the east to continue the ascent of the ridge. It reaches the open ridge top and follows it east for a short spell until it comes to the junction with the Overlook Trail.

The Lost Bay trailhead and dock are 0.9 mile to the south on the Overlook Trail, and the Cruiser Lake Campsite is a 3.6-mile hike to the north.

AGNES LAKE CUTOFF (Distance—0.5 mile): This short trail runs east to west, connecting the Overlook and Cruiser Lake trails. Its west end is located only 0.2 mile south of where the northern half of the Ek Lake Loop terminates on the Overlook Trail.

From the west end the first half of the trail is a level walk through a thick forest of predominantly white spruce. Eventually you begin to see a marsh area to the north and then a pond. At this point the trail dips and climbs a little and the trees thin out until it reaches the junction with the Cruiser Lake Trail.

13 KABETOGAMA PENINSULA

The Cruiser Lake Trail system is the centerpiece of hiking in Voyageurs National Park but by no means the only trails in this water-dominated preserve. There are several other footpaths on the Kabetogama Peninsula and miles of tote roads, and while it would be difficult to link them together for an extended backpacking trip, they do provide opportunities for day hikes or overnight excursions into the interior of this roadless peninsula.

The Locator Lake Trail is best suited for this as it is an overland link between Kabetogama Lake and the shoreline campsite on the inland lake. The 1.6-mile trail is a scenic route, winding past beaver ponds and over three ridges for impressive views. The path is shared by day hikers and paddlers who use it as an alternative to Cranberry Creek for getting in and out of the Chain of Lakes.

Ryan Lake Trail is a 1.1-mile path to the campsite on the inland lake, and the 4.6-mile Kabetogama–Shoepack Lake Trail is a much more challenging route to the south end of the isolated lake. A common day trip from Kabetogama Lake is to hike the first half of the Kabetogama–Shoepack Lake Trail to the abandoned lookout tower for a view of the peninsula's broken terrain.

The Black Bay Ski Trail is a favorite of nordic skiers in the winter, but hikers can also enjoy sections of it that are both scenic and dry during the summer. The Black Bay system is 8.7 miles of loops that offer a range from "easy" to "most

Beaver lodge in Cruiser Lake

difficult" routes for skiers. Hikers can combine the trails to put together a round trip from either the Black Bay access or the entry point off Dove Bay.

Tote roads and old logging trails do not lend themselves to extended hikes. Most should be undertaken without a backpack and with the expectation that you will encounter wetlands and marsh areas. But they do offer challenging hiking and increased opportunities to view wildlife for those with an adventurous spirit and a spare day on their itinerary.

LOCATOR LAKE TRAIL

Distance: 2 miles
Hiking time: 1 hour (one way)
High point: 1210 feet
Rating: moderate   **Map—page 161**

The trail begins 0.75 mile east of La Bontys Point where a dock and VNP sign have been erected near the mouth of an unnamed bay in the northwest corner of Kabetogama Lake. The trailhead was moved in 1985 but canoeists can still paddle into the bay to the old trailhead and cut 0.4 mile of portaging. The trail enters the forest to cross a bridge over a stream and then ascend a low ridge. The highpoint provides good views back across the bay toward Kabetogama Lake. The path continues along the ridge until it reaches the end of a large marsh that contains two beaver ponds. The trail skirts around the ponds but is well planked and provides views of several impressive beaver dams and lodges. Here you have a good chance of sighting a beaver swimming. The trail leaves the ponds and follows a level course for a short distance until it drops steeply into a ravine. It crosses the ravine and begins a climb to the top of the other side along a well-graded section of trail. Even so it is a knee-bending climb, especially if you are hauling a boat.

Once at the top of the ridge the trail follows the rocky crest for the next 0.5 mile and opens up to good views of the ravine that leads northeast into Locator Lake. Eventually the trail descends from this ridge and then climbs up and over two smaller ones before dropping into the center of Locator Lake Campsite.

KABETOGAMA–SHOEPACK LAKE TRAIL

Distance: 4.6 miles
Hiking time: 3–4 hours
High point: 1346 feet
Rating: moderate to difficult   **Map—page 116**

This trail is a favorite of nordic skiers but can also be hiked during the summer. Orange tags mark much of the trail in the first half as it works its way around a series of beaver ponds and wetlands. During the winter, when everything is frozen, this presents no problems for skiers. But in the summer hikers will find themselves tiptoeing across beaver dams and putting extra mileage in as they walk wide around ponds and marsh areas to stay dry. It is highly recommended that hikers tackle the trail with rubber boots rather than conventional hiking boots.

Conditions on the second half are just the opposite—it is a dry, pleasant hike with no wet areas to worry about. An overnight trip is possible as the trail ends behind an old cabin on Shoepack Lake which is surrounded by a grassy field where a tent can be pitched. The water in Shoepack is not desirable for drinking and hikers should carry in their own supply.

The unmarked trail begins on Kabetogama Lake at a shallow cove just west of the Eagle View Campsite cove. From the campsite, head to the western shore of the cove and round the point to the set of cabins on the other side. The trail begins just beyond the one farthest west. During the summer you can actually see it begin in the grass above the rocky shoreline; head for the last cabin and then swing north just before reaching it.

The first 0.3 mile is a gentle climb along an easy-to-follow trail, with marsh areas to the west. Eventually the trail reaches a junction with a logging trail that splits off to the west through the marsh area. The Shoepack Lake Trail continues north and soon breaks out at the first of many beaver ponds along the way. Skiers can go straight across, but hikers have to turn west and use an old beaver dam to cross over, then cut back to the trail on the other side of the pond.

From here the trail becomes a dry path as it climbs a high point and then quickly drops to the other side to another beaver pond. Summer hikers can again cross this one by using a beaver dam to the west. Once on the other side of the pond the trail resumes with a climb to 1205 feet and then drops steeply to a beaver pond north of the small ridge.

The trail ends right at the foot of a dam, and both skiers and hikers can cross it and then look to the east to find the path on the other side. It resumes as a dry path in the summer but quickly drops to another wet area bordered on one side by rock bluffs. The trail curves before the high rocks and then crosses a stream where an orange tag can be seen on the other side.

Once on the other side of the stream you will arrive at another pond and dam. Cross the dam and skirt the pond toward the east end for a few yards. You will come to a second dam and as you tiptoe across this one you should spot an orange tag on the other side. The trail resumes here on solid ground and follows the east end of the pond before swinging north into the woods. Winter travelers have it lucky as they can just cross the frozen pond and skip crossing the dams: ski or snowshoe the length of the pond toward its west end, and just before reaching it look for a break in the trees along the north shore.

Both hikers and skiers return to the trail, which continues north along a path that is surprisingly dry during the summer, considering the marsh area it cuts through. Eventually it breaks out at a beaver pond, and again skiers can go straight across and look among the trees for the trail to resume. Hikers don't have it so easy—this is the last marsh and pond area that the trail crosses, but it's also the wettest. Summer hikers do best by swinging to the west before slogging through it.

The trail continues through a stand of pine north of the pond and then arrives at a semiopen area before returning to the forest for the last time. This is a joyous point for summer hikers, as the trail is dry and easy to follow from here to the end. The next 0.4 mile is a gentle climb through predominantly aspen and birch forest before the trail peaks out at a ridge top with scattered pine.

The trail descends and then climbs again, this time peaking out at the junction with the spur to the Shoepack lookout tower. A faded wooden sign points the way, and the tower is 0.3 mile to the west along a trail that crosses mostly bare rock and during the summer can be confusing. The tower is built 1364 feet above sea level, the highest point on the Kabetogama Peninsula, and it's a climb of 64

Old fire tower near Shoepack Lake

rungs to reach the top. The views are worth it, however, as you can see much of the peninsula and as far north as Rainy Lake.

The main trail departs north of the junction and quickly passes a beaver pond to the east before beginning a segment that follows the broken terrain for the next 0.7 mile. Eventually the trail makes the final 0..5-mile descent to Shoepack Lake, where it bottoms out to cross a small stream and pass another beaver pond before breaking out into the grassy area behind the old cabin.

Those paddlers who entered Shoepack Lake from another route and want to hike to the lookout tower can walk behind the cabin and follow the line of trees that borders the grassy area to the south. The trail can be seen among the trees, 30 yards from the cabin.

RYAN LAKE TRAIL

Distance: 1.1 miles
Hiking time: 30–45 minutes
High point: 1150 feet
Rating: moderate to difficult   Map—page 137

The trailhead for the Ryan Lake Trail is located 1.5 miles east of Anderson Bay on Rainy Lake, directly south of a Virgin Island campsite (see chapter 11). It begins on the west side of the stream that flows from Ryan Lake into Rainy Lake. The VNP sign that marks the beginning lists the trail as 0.8 mile long, but the actual hike to the campsite is 1.1 miles.

From Rainy Lake the trail heads south and soon comes to what appears to be a Y junction. The fork to the west is an overgrown tote road that ends at a small cove. The trail swings to the east, crosses a small stream, and then begins a gradual climb as it returns to its southern course. At one point the trail levels out and passes a marsh area to the west where the stream flows into Ryan Lake. Here paddlers can end the hike by putting their boats in and heading for the lake.

The trail resumes climbing and reaches a bushy slope that overlooks the north end of the lake. Parts of the trail in this section might be overgrown and difficult to follow at times, but the trail hugs the ridge and does not drop to the water. After 50 yards the trail descends with the ridge, not toward the shoreline, and then climbs up and over a second ridge.

From here the trail stays close to the pine-covered shoreline of Ryan Lake and winds back to the lower half of the lake to end at a rocky point where the campsite is situated. From the bushy slope at the north end of the lake to the campsite, a series of faded blue dots has been placed on trees to assist hikers in locating the trail.

RYAN LAKE AND CAMPSITE: The table and stand-up grill of the campsite are located on a rock slab that extends into the lake for a splendid view of the entire body of water. A pit toilet is provided, but good tent space is limited and the spot could be buggy from late July through early August. Apart from that, the campsite is a gem that will provide a pleasant experience away from all other users of the park, including other hikers and paddlers.

Ryan Lake, which measures 0.6 mile in length and less than 0.25 mile at its widest point, is a very scenic body of water with its high bluffs along the west shore. Anglers will find the fishing good for northern pike and smallmouth bass.

Swamp in middle of Kabetogama Peninsula

BLACK BAY SKI TRAIL

Distance: 8.7 miles (round trip from Black Bay to Dove Bay)
Hiking time: 3–5 hours
High point: 1180 feet
Rating: moderate to difficult

The Black Bay Ski Trail was designed and built for nordic skiers and offers a series of loops that range from easy tours to more challenging routes. The trail system is basically a figure-eight route between Black Bay and Dove Bay with an additional 2.4-mile trail that loops above it. Summer hikers will find the figure-eight portion a reasonably dry route with only a few wetlands to cross. The 2.4-mile trail to the north can be extremely wet during the summer—almost impassable at times.

You can gain access to the trail in the winter by driving 0.5 mile along the ice road to the Black Bay trailhead or 4 miles to the Dove Bay end. During the summer, hikers can paddle from the public ramp on Island View to the Black Bay trailhead in 20 to 30 minutes under normal conditions. The trails will be described in the one-way direction that skiers must follow.

"EASY" LOOP (Distance: 0.9 mile): A large VNP sign marks the west end of the Black Bay Ski Trail along Black Bay Narrows. The beginning of the trail is situated in a clearing where a ranger information hut, map box, and pit toilets are located. The trail departs east from here and during the summer looks more like a 6-foot wide clearing in the trees than a footpath. It follows a very level course for a short way and then comes to the first junction. The fork to northeast (left) is part of the "more difficult" loop that reaches Dove Bay in 3 miles.

The "easy" loop is the fork to the southeast (right), with the trail continuing on its level course. The loop curves to the south, where it comes to the junction with the "more difficult" loop returning from Dove Bay. Here the "easy" loop swings to the west and in the summer the next 0.5 mile will be a grassy area harboring strawberry patches. Gradually the loop swings to the north, where it enters an open area and crosses to the trailhead and ranger hut on the shores of Black Bay Narrows.

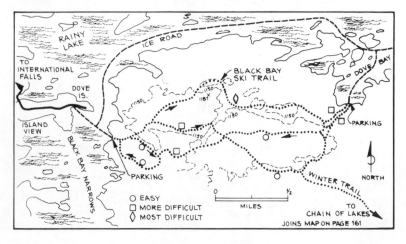

Black Bay Ski Trail (Steve Maass photo)

"MORE DIFFICULT" LOOP (Distance: 5.8 miles): This trail departs from the "easy" loop 0.25 mile from the Black Bay Narrows trailhead and is the northeast fork marked with yellow tags, signifying that it is "more difficult" for skiers. It begins by ascending slightly and then leveling out in 0.25 mile, where it reaches a junction with the "most difficult" trail. The "more difficult" loop is the trail to the right. It heads east, where it ascends slightly and then follows a path through the trees, dipping and climbing slightly for the next 0.25 mile. Eventually it breaks out into a clearing, where to the south is a view of a large beaver pond.

The yellow trail hugs the ridge to the east end of the pond, where it enters a sparsely forested area and arrives at a short cut. A posted sign points the way to an easier path for skiers. Summer hikers should follow the more challenging route as it will be slightly drier. Both paths descend and cross a lowland section that will be wet in the summer but manageable with rubber boots.

From the wet area the trail climbs to the major junction of the "more difficult" loop, the middle of the figure eight located 1.5 miles from the Black Bay Narrows. The junction is the site of a table, pit toilets, and three other forks. Skiers can head southeast along an "easy" trail to Dove Bay 2 miles away or 1.4 miles southwest on a return trip to the trailhead at Black Bay Narrows. The third fork departs almost due east and is the 1.2-mile, one-way trail from Dove Bay to the junction.

The eastern half of the figure eight is rated as "easy" and marked with blue tags. Following the southeast fork the trail wanders in the woods for a short distance before ascending to a view of a beaver pond. It reenters the forest only to emerge at another beaver pond surrounded by an open marsh area. From here the trail returns to the trees and swings due east. It dips and climbs for the next

0.5 mile before making a rapid ascent. After peaking out, the trail swings north and follows this course until it comes to the junction with the Dove Bay spur.

The spur departs northeast, reaching Dove Bay in 0.5 mile, while the northwest fork loops back to Black Bay Narrows, 2.2 miles away. The spur is a rapid descent to the bay, skirting a beaver pond and passing an osprey nest perched in a dead tree along the way. Paralleling it near the end is the one-way spur that heads from the trailhead back to the main loop. This 0.25-mile trail makes a steady ascent and joins the northern loop, the "most difficult" trail, as it swings into the figure-eight portion of the trail system. At this point Black Bay Narrows lies 2.3 miles away for skiers along the "easy" and "more difficult" loops. Hikers could choose to return along the northern loop, but would find it extremely wet during the summer.

From the junction with the spur the "most difficult" trail descends south into a lowland area that will be wet but manageable during the summer before climbing out of it and joining the "easy" loop at a winter rest area with a table and grill. At this point the "easy" loop heads west and follows this course for the next 0.75 mile as it dips and climbs gently, crossing only a few wet areas during the summer.

The trail curves to the south just before reaching the table and pit toilets at the junction with the "more difficult" loop. Skiers take the southwest fork and follow the 1-mile section of the yellow trail as it makes a gradual descent into a lowland area. Hikers will find this spot wet in the summer, but will return to dryer footing when the trail ascends on the other side. Shortly after leaving the wet area, the trail curves sharply to the north and then again to the west. From here it descends into the "easy" loop, which both skiers and hikers can follow 0.4 mile back to the Black Bay Narrows trailhead (see description above).

"MOST DIFFICULT" LOOP (Distance: 2.4 miles): The "most difficult" loop is marked with red tags and skiers will find it the most challenging route of the Black Bay Ski Trail. Hikers will discover large, often impassable wet areas along it. During the winter it follows a one-way direction from west to east beginning at a junction 0.5 mile up the "more difficult" loop from the Black Bay Narrows trailhead.

The red trail swings to the north and dips and climbs gently for the first 0.5 mile through thick forest along a ridge. It makes a steady and at times rapid descent off the ridge into a lowland area that is extremely wet during the summer and impassable after a recent thunderstorm. The trail climbs out of the wet area up a small ridge and then descends it by making a sharp swing to the south.

The trail follows a somewhat level course south for 0.25 mile before climbing again and swinging to the east. From here the red trail climbs up and over three ridges in the next 0.75 mile before descending sharply toward Dove Bay. Just as the trail levels out it curves to the south, where it makes a sharp ascent past the one-way spur from Dove Bay to the next spur immediately following it that leads to the trailhead. The red trail continues south, where it joins the "easy" loop on the eastern half of the figure eight.

TOTE ROADS

Tote roads are old logging trails that were cut in the 1920s and '30s to enable loggers to move the fallen trees from the middle of the Kabetogama Peninsula to the frozen outer lakes. This was done with horse teams and sleds in the middle of the winter over trails that usually traversed frozen swamps or lowlands. While such routes still provide good conditions for winter travel by ski, snowshoe, or snowmobile, in the summer they are definitely a hiker's challenge.

The roads are labeled on USGS topographicals as "winter trails," but the maps are often misleading when you are studying them to find a tote road to follow. Some you will never locate, as they have long since been taken over by aspen and birch forests. Others resemble a wide jeep trail, with a pair of tracks running deep into the peninsula for a couple of miles—only to deadend at a beaver pond.

Describing the roads is almost impossible as they are in constant flux. Dry weather will make them considerably easier to find and follow, but beavers have the ability to wipe out entire sections of a tote road with one dam. Aspen saplings can hide a trail in no time, and a white-tailed deer, foraging on the new growth, can reopen the route.

The fun in hiking, snowshoeing, or skiing tote roads is to use your backcountry instinct along with your map and compass in an attempt to follow them. To be able to read the terrain and know where you are and where you're going is a challenge to experienced backpackers. The old trails can also lead to increased encounters with wildlife. Permanent residents of the peninsula, such as deer, black bears, and moose, also travel along them or often can be seen feeding on the aspen or brush.

Listed below are just four tote roads or "winter trails" within the park. These trails are easy to locate and can be followed at least part of the way even during the summer. All should be considered challenging journeys in either the summer or winter.

Black Bay to Locator Lake

A tote road runs from the most easterly inlet of Black Bay to Locator Lake, 2.7 miles to the east. Paddlers staying at Locator Lake Campsite can hike much of it from east to west or pick up the snowmobile trail in the middle of it to reach the bay off of Kabetogama Lake formed by La Bontys Point. The eastern end can

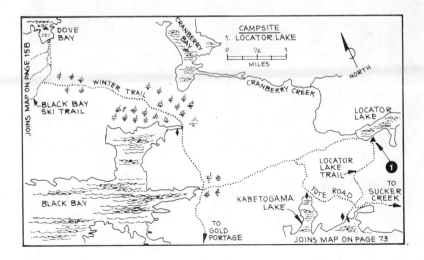

Old tote road (logging road) now used by skiers and adventurous hikers

be reached by following the edge of the ridge that borders the beginning of Cranberry Creek to the south. Skiers can depart from the southwest "easy" loop of the Black Bay Ski Trail to pick up a winter trail that leads to its western end just off the inlet. The route is a popular one for weekend snowmobilers headed for the Chain of Lakes.

La Bontys Point to Sucker Creek (Map—page 73)

From the back of the bay inside La Bontys Point a wide trail departs east and crosses the base of the peninsula to the next bay, where the Locator Lake trailhead and dock are located. From here the trail skirts the bay and cuts through a marsh area and stream before climbing over a ridge and dropping to the inlet opposite the mouth of Sucker Creek, 2.3 miles from the bay formed by La Bontys Point. Much of the route from the Locator Lake trailhead to the east is lost in the marsh area or in aspen growth, though skiers and snowshoers would have few problems completing it. The east end near Sucker Creek can be located by paddling into the inlet and looking for the pair of structures that appear to be old wells. From here travel in a northwest direction through the brush, which will quickly give way to a wide tote road.

Clyde Creek Loop (Map—page 69)

A pair of tote roads form a loop between Clyde Creek and the bay to the north of Nashata Point. The trail is easily located from the bay as it swings south off a ridge almost to the water before curving to the east and cutting through the grassy clearing to cross a stream in the back. Heading east on the trail you will arrive at a junction in 1.3 miles. Here the Clyde Creek Loop swings to the northwest and in less than 0.5 mile passes some extensive beaver ponds. Another tote road continues east from the junction toward Deer Creek. The trail is more difficult to find from Clyde Creek. The entire loop would make a challenging hike of over 6 miles.

Mica Bay to Namakan Lake (Map—page 105)

This snowmobile route begins halfway along the south shore of Mica Bay and heads south for 2 miles to the Namakan Lake shoreline just north of the entrance to Johnson Bay. Hikers can easily locate either end, but can follow only a portion of it in the summer before they are stopped by extensive ponds and marshes.

14 MAINLAND TRAILS

On the American mainland that surrounds the large outside lakes of Voyageurs National Park there are several trails that can be hiked, snowshoed, or skied. Three of them lie inside the park and the other two in the Kabetogama State Forest. Although none of them is long enough to be used for an extended backpacking trip during the summer, they all depart from the beaten path or busy waterways for a challenging hike into the interior woods.

The most interesting one is the route to Lucille Lake from Browns Bay. The route is ideal for those undertaking their first cross-country hike since it is only 2 miles one-way across ridges of smooth granite to the scenic lake deep in the heart of the park. The Lucille Lake route can be turned into an overnight side trip, highlighted by fishing in a body of water reached by only a few hikers each summer.

The Ash River Falls Trail system lies just outside the park within Kabetogama State Forest. The 12.5 miles of loops provide hiking opportunities in the summer and groomed and tracked nordic ski trails in the winter that range from easy to most difficult.

The other three trails are not maintained and present challenging conditions for backcountry travelers. They are best tackled by snowshoers in the winter as they involve extensive wetlands and swamps. They include the former Mukooda Ski Trail just west of the lake of the same name; Daly Bay Trail, which departs from the Ash River Trail road north to Kabetogama Lake; and the Hoist Bay Trail that links Ash River to Hoist Bay.

LUCILLE LAKE ROUTE

Distance: 2 miles
Hiking time:1–2 hours (one way)
High point: 1370 feet
Rating: moderate

There has been talk by VNP rangers of building a trail from Browns Bay to Lucille Lake and hikers entering the park should check to see whether such a path has been laid. Until it is built, the journey to the scenic little lake is a cross-country hike that follows a semiopen route along the bare, rocky backs of two major ridges. There is some climbing involved but the hike is not difficult—it is ideal for a person's first attempt at traveling in the woods where no trail exists.

If you made a direct line from Browns Bay to Lucille Lake, it would measure 1.8 miles. But few hikes are that exact and most people usually end up walking more than 2 miles before they reach the shore of the lake. Numerous rock cairns have been placed along the ridges by the handful of visitors who attempt the route each summer. The route markers serve as reassurance that you are traveling in the right direction, but don't be alarmed when they suddenly disappear. Too many hikers have set up too many cairns to mark a single route. It is better to base your direction of travel on map and compass readings than on a rock cairn.

The best place to start is directly across from the rounded peninsula at the northeast corner of Browns Bay. When paddling south along the west shore, pass the first four coves from the entrance of the bay until you come to a stone islet just beyond the fourth one. At this point the rock bluffs come right down to the water and you can begin ascending them south of the islet.

The route begins with a climb of the rock bluff and then switches to a level hike through a wooded area at the top. After a short distance you will be confronted by a steep ridge which will require a little scrambling to scale it. Once at the top resume the due west course.

At this point the trees begin to thin out and one long stretch of bare rock after another will appear, all polished smooth by glaciers 10,000 years ago. They are broken up by small stands of trees but the underbrush will be light and you should spot another stretch of bare rock to the west. The hiking is easy along this section and the scenery fascinating. Between the slabs of granite, there will be pockets of wildflowers bursting with color. The most commonly seen ones are eastern columbine, wild rose, and the magnificent lady's slipper, which can be spotted growing several in a bunch. One of the largest members of the orchid family, the lady's slipper blooms in early summer and is easy to spot by its pink bulbous sac, which can grow to 2.5 inches in length.

Gradually the ridge top ascends until it peaks at a high point of 1350 to 1370 feet above sea level almost a mile from the bay. Here the terrain levels out somewhat, and eventually you should come to the west side of the ridge you have been crossing. It should be a noticeably steep drop, but if you come to a high cliff overlooking swamp and marsh area you have wandered too far north. If that is the case it is best to follow the side of the ridge south before descending from it.

After descending the ridge you will come to another long, smooth section of rock running north to south followed by a forest sprinkled with small wet areas. This should last only a short distance before a second ridge appears and more stretches of bare rock. On this ridge you will drop into a thick growth of trees and then return to its crest and the open areas of rock. If your line of direction has been consistent, and your luck good, you will remain in this type of terrain right up until you see the lake's shimmering surface. At this point you hack your way a hundred yards through thick brush to Lucille's shoreline. If you wander too far south the last 0.25 mile or even more will be forest and thick underbrush.

LUCILLE LAKE: The lake is 0.75 mile long and 0.5 mile at its widest point toward the north end. Its clear water has a maximum depth of 19 feet, and those who reach it with fishing poles should find good action for northern pike and

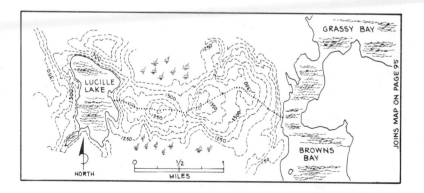

smallmouth bass. The best camping spot for hikers lies on the small peninsula toward the southeast corner of the lake. Hikers who maintain a due west course will break out on the shoreline near the point and need only skirt the lake's shoreline a short distance to reach it.

ASH RIVER FALLS TRAIL SYSTEM

Distance: 12.5 miles (all loops)
High point: 1390 feet
Rating: easy to difficult

The first of two parking areas for the trail system lies 5.2 miles east of US 53 on the Ash River Trail road (County Road 129). The parking area is north of the road and has an information board near the trailhead. From here the trail heads south, crossing the road in 0.25 mile where skiers and hikers have a choice of trails. Loop A consists of "easy" and "more difficult" ski trails that depart southwest to the banks of the river. To the southeast is Loop B, with "more difficult" and "most difficult" ski trails that climb and follow a large ridge to the east.

From the second parking lot on the south side of Ash River Trail road, the trail begins with an ascent to the open ridge east of where you left your car. Once at the top the trail begins a gradual descent that quickly becomes steeper. This is followed by a sharp swing to the south and a rapid drop-off until the trail bottoms out in a clearcut area. From here it cuts east through the clearcut, begins

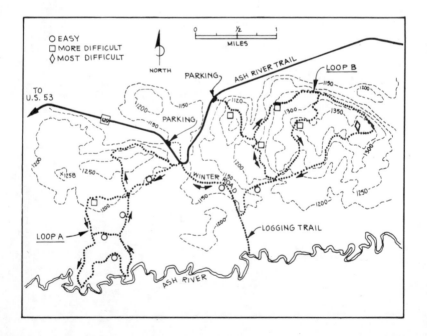

an ascent, and arrives at a junction in the middle of the western trail of Loop B 0.7 mile from the parking area.

Summer hikers find that the best trails to follow are either Loop B or the top half of Loop A, which avoid the extensive wet areas that surround the Ash River.

LOOP B TRAILS (Distance: 6.9 miles): Loop B begins as a winter road from the junction with Loop A along the Ash River Trail road and for the first 1.2 miles traverses a fairly level and sometimes wet route. Eventually it begins to climb slightly and arrives at a junction with several forks. The trail curves sharply to the north at this point and is marked with a posted map. Opposite the trail is a continuation of the winter road that heads south to Ash River.

From the junction the trail becomes a wide path that remains level but in the summer can be wet. After 0.25 mile it ascends slightly to a junction with three forks where an adirondack hut has been built. Skiers must take the fork that departs to the northwest since the other two loops are one-way trails from the northern edge of the ridge back to the warming hut.

The western loop, or outer loop as it is commonly known, is 1.5 miles long and rated "more difficult." It begins by winding through a thick forest along a level route. In a little over 0.5 mile the trail descends noticeably and arrives at a junction with the cutoff trail that leads 0.7 mile northwest to the second parking area along Ash River Trail road. The western loop continues by swinging to the northeast and beginning with a short descent that makes for a good downhill run in the winter. From here it is a steady climb to the top of the ridge's northern edge, where the trail eventually arrives at a junction with the central and eastern loops.

At the top of the ridge the thick aspen and spruce forest gives way to frequent clearings and you are rewarded with a scenic view of the valley to the north. Departing from the junction is the central loop, 1.25 miles long and rated "more difficult," and the eastern loop, 2.1 miles and rated "most difficult." The central loop winds south through open areas that will be snow-covered clearings in the winter and bare rock patches in the summer before ascending another crest in the ridge. From here it dips and climbs through more open areas while curving gradually to the southwest.

Eventually the trail takes a sharp swing to the south and begins a gradual 0.7-mile descent to the warming hut. A half-mile from the hut the trail curves to the southwest.

The eastern loop is rated as "most difficult," but the long runs downhill, if taken with caution, do not demand an advanced level of skiing ability. The trail is marked by a series of blue diamonds that lead east from the main junction along the northern edge of the ridge. The trail dips and rises along the back of the ridge, staying in the cover of a thick forest. After 0.25 mile the trail curves to the north and then curves again to views of the valley and the ridge that forms its north side. From here the trees thin out and summer hikers with sharp eyes will be rewarded with lowbush cranberries and blueberries.

The trail follows the open ridge top for the next 0.5 mile, with a steady view of the valley below—this is a scenic section winter or summer. Three-quarters of a mile from the junction the trail curves sharply to the south, leaving the views behind and ascending gradually. The trail swings to the west in a short distance and dips and climbs over a rocky section of the ridge before making another sharp turn to the south. At this point it makes a rapid descent before swinging to the southwest and leveling off. The final leg is a level hike or straight ski to the warming hut and junction with the two other loops.

Once back at the warming hut you can return to your starting point either by backtracking along the winter road 1.6 miles to the parking lot or by following the western loop and the cutoff 1.4 miles to the second parking lot. From one parking area to the other it is a 1.1-mile hike along Ash River Trail road.

LOOP A TRAILS (Distance: 5.6 miles): This loop trail is fairly flat except for the northern portion, which climbs a ridge and provides nordic skiers with several long downhill runs. Hikers will enjoy a dry route along most of this segment, the northern half of the figure eight, but will discover cedar swamps that make for a wet stretch in the southern loops.

From the Ash River Trail road, Loop A departs to the southwest and in 200 yards comes to its first junction, marked by a posted map. Skiers must follow the southern fork. Hikers who take the northwest trail will quickly ascend the ridge to scenic views at its crest. The trail to the south departs from the junction and descends slightly, bottoming out in a cedar swamp where in the winter it is often possible to view the tracks of white-tailed deer, pine martin, fisher, weasel, and even wolf.

Skier checks out maps along the Ash River Ski Trail (Steve Maass photo)

The trail climbs slightly and in 0.6 mile from the road passes the junction in the middle of the figure eight. The trail to the north winds 1.3 miles up the ridge before curving back to Ash River Trail road. Due south is the one-way trail back from Ash River, but skiers follow the one-way loop to the southwest, which is rated "more difficult." The trail makes a short ascent to the top of a small ridge and then descends its south side into a large cedar swamp, a very quiet and peaceful place in the still of the winter. Travelers should keep an eye out for browsing deer in this area.

After crossing the flat, evergreen-studded swamp area the trail passes a junction with a short cutoff that extends 0.3 mile to the east side of the loop. From the junction the trail leaves the swamp area and enters a section of open ash forest and then descends to the bank of the Ash River. The level trail swings away from the river, returns to it, and then takes a sharp turn north where you cross cedar swamp, passing the short cutoff trail at one point.

A half-mile after passing the cutoff trail you enter an aspen-birch-spruce forest and arrive at the major junction of the figure eight loop. The 1.3-mile trail that departs north is rated "more difficult." It begins with a gradual climb up the ridge and enters an open jack pine forest at the top. Good views of the neighboring ridge to the north will greet you as the trail swings to the east. The trail ends with several exciting downhill runs, a short climb, and one final gradual downhill section that ends at the short spur to Ash River Trail road.

MUKOODA SKI TRAIL

Distance: 7.6 miles
High point: 1270 feet
Rating: difficult

Map—page 95

In 1984 the VNP rangers decided to no longer maintain the Mukooda Ski Trail and to remove the markers and signposts along the route. But while the trail signs might be gone, the route will remain for years to come and will be a challenge for experienced backpackers to follow in either summer or winter. Access to it during the winter is 2 miles north along the ice road from Crane Lake. At this point the road crosses the neck of land to Mukooda Lake but nordic skiers or snowshoers should follow the shoreline of the large bay that marks the north end of Crane Lake. It is 1 mile from the ice road to the back of the bay where the main loop of the trail swings near the shoreline.

The best access point during the summer is along the west shore of Mukooda Lake. Paddle to the island that lies farthest to the south and then to the shoreline directly west of it. Scramble 20 yards up the ridge and you will encounter the trail.

The southern loop is a 3.25-mile circle that passes through an extensive swamp area in its southwest corner. The northern loop is 3.3 miles long and departs and returns to the southern loop. Just beyond the eastern junction between the two trails, the northern loop cuts through an extensive wetland that is often impassable during the summer.

Summer hikers will find the best traveling along the eastern half of the southern loop and along the western half of both loops, where the trail follows the top of a ridge. You can reach this scenic section during the summer by hiking the southern loop north from Mukooda Lake where it takes a sharp swing west and

On the Ash River Ski Trail (Steve Maass photo)

passes one end of the northern loop. From here it is a little over 0.5 mile until you come to the T-junction where the two loops meet again, and dry hiking will be found along either fork. Eventually, however, summer hikers will encounter more swamp areas and should be prepared for them by wearing 14-inch rubber boots.

ASH RIVER–HOIST BAY TRAIL

Distance: 2.5 miles
High point: 1150 feet
Rating: easy   **Map—page 82**

The Ash River–Hoist Bay Trail begins where a small stream empties into the east side of the river's entrance, across from the last series of resorts on the west bank. At this point the bed of the former Virginia & Rainy Lake railroad line that hauled logs from Hoist Bay can be followed. It heads northeast and crosses a narrow inlet at the north end of Moose River and then the river itself, where the pilings of the former railroad bridge still stand. The electric lines point the way on the other side of the Moose River, and you can follow them along the south end of Moose Bay, through a large beaver pond and marsh area and as they curve north toward Hoist Bay. The lines lead to the back of the former resort and YCC camp on the bay, where more evidence of the logging era remains.

During the winter, skiers and showshoers will have few problems following the trail but must share it with snowmobilers. During the summer it is used primarily by paddlers portaging their boats from Ash River over to Moose Bay. Hikers without boats have almost no way to cross either Ash River or Moose River.

DALEY BAY SKI TRAIL

Distance: 5.6 miles
High point: 1210 feet
Rating: difficult   **Map—page 62**

The Daley Bay Ski Trail is marked on many maps as a winter trail or cross-country ski route. A winter route, yes. But a nordic ski route? Hardly. It would be just as hard a struggle for skiers to follow it in the winter as it would be for hikers in the summer. The trail, which can be located at each end and is marked with a faded series of orange tags, is for those with an adventurous spirit and a good pair of snowshoes.

The south end of the trail is located 3.8 miles east along the Ash River Trail road and appears as an old tote road with a stack of deteriorating logs near it. The north end can be found behind a group of old cabins on a small cove 1 mile east of Nebraska Bay or just south of Twin Islands in Kabetogama Lake. Summer hikers would find the first 1.5 miles from Ash River Trail road a level, wet walk through heavy brush and aspen saplings until they arrive at one of the two long inlets that mark the south end of Daley Bay. Crossing or fording the waterway would be extremely difficult without extensive planning.

Winter travelers would find the remaining 4.1 miles a struggle through heavy brush along a poorly marked trail where the scenery is less than inspiring.

AFTERWORD

IN THE HEARTS OF VOYAGEURS

I'm not sure how long the old man had been sitting there. I had already made two trips from Jorgens Lake to Eks Bay, where I dropped my packs 3 feet from the water and immediately retraced my steps. On my third journey I emerged from the woods with a kayak over my head and struggled to the sandy shore of the bay. I didn't spot him until I flipped the boat into the water and began to rub my aching shoulders. But when I looked up there he was, sitting offshore in his small runabout, watching me with interest.

He smiled and said, "You must be French Canadian."

I was stunned and for the first time that afternoon I forgot about my throbbing shoulders. "I am. How did you know?"

"There is a little voyageur in your blood, son."

I guess there is. I guess there is a little voyageur in all of us. And when you go to the park that bears the paddler's name it is not hard to feel what the voyageur must have felt, to cherish what he loved, to survive the waterways that he mastered.

Voyageurs National Park is the steep cliffs of Anderson Bay, the stormy beauty of Rainy Lake, the black bear rambling over a ridge in the middle of the Kabetogama Peninsula. But pervading it all is the spirit of its namesakes. The birchbark canoes and red caps have long since vanished from the border lakes. But the energetic love of the North Woods and the enthusiasm for the challenges that lie in the wilderness have remained. They are evident today in every backpacker who paddles, portages, hikes, or slogs in Voyageurs National Park.

(Opposite) Locator Lake

BIBLIOGRAPHY

Interpretive Article Series, International Falls, MN: Voyageurs National Park.

Loegering, W. Q. and E. P. DuCharme. *Plants of the Canoe Country,* 1978.

National Park Service. *Final Environmental Statement,* Denver, CO: U.S. Department of the Interior, 1979.

National Park Service. *Voyageurs National Park Master Plan,* International Falls, MN: Voyageurs National Park, 1980.

Nute, Grace Lee. *Rainy River Country,* St. Paul, MN: The Minnesota Historical Society, 1950.

————. *The Voyageur's Highway,* St. Paul, MN: The Minnesota Historical Society, 1965.

————. *The Voyageur,* New York, NY: D. Appleton and Company, 1931.

Trees of Minnesota. St. Paul, MN: Department of Natural Resources, 1977.

Treuer, Robert. *Voyageur Country: A Park in the Wilderness,* Minneapolis, MN: The University of Minnesota Press, 1979.

INDEX

JIM DUFRESNE is a Saginaw-based writer who specializes in wilderness trips and outdoor adventures. He has hiked extensively in the Upper Midwest, the Rockies and throughout Alaska, as well as in New Zealand, Australia and Nepal. His earlier books include *Isle Royale National Park* (The Mountaineers), *Tramping in New Zealand,* and *Alaska: A Travel Survival Kit.*